When the Cat Had My Tongue

When the Cat Had My Tongue

A Very English Memoir

Diana Fassino

For my new friend
Jean
with very best wishes
Diana Fassino

iUniverse, Inc.
New York Lincoln Shanghai

When the Cat Had My Tongue
A Very English Memoir

Copyright © 2006 by Diana Fassino

iUniverse books may be ordered through booksellers or by contacting:

iUniverse
2021 Pine Lake Road, Suite 100
Lincoln, NE 68512
www.iuniverse.com
1-800-Authors (1-800-288-4677)

Cover painting and pen & ink drawings by the author

ISBN-13: 978-0-595-39615-3 (pbk)
ISBN-13: 978-0-595-84018-2 (ebk)
ISBN-10: 0-595-39615-1 (pbk)
ISBN-10: 0-595-84018-3 (ebk)

Printed in the United States of America

Special Thanks to
my husband Dick for his encouragement
and his computer skills,
to Betsy Pearson for her advice and support,
and to my mentor and guru, John Whitney

For the Beloveds: Jane, Ming, Steve and Rob
Tania, Chimo, Oliver, and Serena
And for Johnny and Tom and their five daughters
And Iris's four sons and daughters
And for Dick, my darling Professor Higgins

"Nanny, what's 'in the family way'?"

"Ask no questions you'll hear no lies.
Eat up those crusts. They'll make your hair curl."

Contents

Preface xiii

1   A Close Call 1

2   Blame it on the Black Bottom 6

3   Two Grannies 15

4   The Big House 20

5   Rare Events 35

6   War Baby 44

7   Horse Heaven and Hunting Hell 56

8   Village Life 66

9   Seldom Seen or Heard 79

10   The Pied Piper of Edwinstowe 94

11   Uprooted 105

12   Banished 112

13   Jinxed 120

14   Swiss Miss 133

15   Falling in Love with Love? 141

16   Who's Afraid of the Big Bad Wolf? 149

17   On the Shelf 158

18   Love's Young Dream? 165

19   Postscript 179

A Recent Gathering of the Beloveds 185

About the Author 187

Preface

My grandmother in Yorkshire covered all the mirrors in the vicarage during thunder storms, went shopping in a gig drawn by a dappled grey horse, and viewed the advent of electricity with grave suspicion. My son flew his helicopter far up into the icy wastes of the high Arctic. My wild and wonderful grandchildren in Maui, armed with their ubiquitous cell phones and iPods, toss their surf boards into the backs of trucks as big as elephants and roar off to answer the siren call of the mighty rolling ocean.

The man in the moon is no longer a nursery rhyme character, there are people walking about with other peoples' hearts beating in their chests and hips made of titanium, the tomato in your salad may contain fish genes, and the Internet has cast a glittering web of knowledge and information around our world.

But of all the changes I've witnessed in my lifetime, perhaps none astonishes me more than the role of modern children, who have stepped out of the wings, high-jacked the spotlight, and seized centre-stage as their birthright. In stark contrast, I grew up in a world where children were 'seen and not heard', where asking questions was frowned upon, and there was no one to tell about nighttime terrors concerning the monster that lurked under the bed. I suppose in the circumstances it's hardly surprising that on the rare occasion when some grownup spoke to me or asked me a question Nanny would reply on my behalf, "The cat's got her tongue."

I didn't find my voice till I was about forty, but I did apparently become the keeper of my family's story which, with love and a few laughs and tears, I am returning to them now within the pages of this book. I offer it too, to anyone interested in those long-ago times of innocence, when it seems the sun always shone on summer holidays, animals were allowed to peck and root about in farmyards, television was a mere rumour, a half-penny would buy a twirly stick of barley sugar, Robin Hood still lived in Sherwood Forest, and Hitler's face was—oh how rude!—printed on the lavatory paper.

So turn off the electronics, take my hand, and come with me to spend an hour or two in that nostalgic and enchanted land known as "the olden days."

Chapter 1

A Close Call

"Look here," said Sir William, "You really cannot go around hanging the village children. You are privileged children. Do you know what that means?"

"But Our-Edly's our enemy," said my brother Johnny. "Like Hitler."

I knew who Hitler was because a recent windfall among the new wartime shortages had been a whole case of lavatory paper, the thin, scratchy sheets printed with cartoons of Herr Hitler which we children thought wonderfully rude and funny.

"Best place for the little swine," said our father.

Johnny and I, the children from The Big House, were heavily outnumbered in our battles with the village boys when they ignored the No Trespassing signs and came with jam jars swinging jauntily from string handles to fish for minnows in our stream or to pick blackberries or throw stones at our ponies. We were always trailing home soaked to the skin or covered with bramble scratches from these encounters, so it had been a rare coup to capture their leader, ginger-haired foul-mouthed Our-Edly.

Fortunately for him, Nanny's voice had come floating across the misty evening garden from the nursery window calling us in to tea, so we'd had to abandon him, trussed up and balanced on a wobbly apple crate with a rope round his neck hitched to a cross-beam in the ponies' shed.

"Well, lucky for you no real harm was done," said Sir William. Apparently he'd been passing as darkness fell and gone to investigate sobs and curses coming from the shed. (Imagine the legal fall-out today.) "Off you go now, but just remember this," he added sternly, "with privilege comes responsibility to those less fortunate than yourselves."

"Yes, Sir William," said Johnny.

On a waft of *Quelques Fleurs* our mother was descending
the sweeping curved staircase into the hall

"Yes, Sir William," I echoed, though I couldn't imagine what he meant. Our-Edly and his gang were less fortunate than us? Clearly Sir William didn't know how much we craved their diet of bread and dripping and fish and chips and envied then their obviously rare encounters with soap and water. I even envied them the way the cosy prefix "Our" was attached to everyone's names in the village. I would have loved to be "Our-Diana." There was no six o'clock bedtime for Our-Edly and his gang, or boring Sunday mornings spent fidgeting in the family pew at church, and their acts of vandalism and clashes with authority gave them, in our eyes, the glamour of revolutionaries. I put the puzzling idea of being 'privileged' away to think about some other time.

Sir William was our favourite grown-up person. I know now that he was also almost certainly our mother's lover. But those were more discrete times, and so far as I know they were never found out.

"Hope he won't tell Daddy," muttered Johnny as we scuffled to be first out of the drawing room door, colliding with Violet the parlour maid, who was already tottering under the weight of the vast clinking silver cocktail tray. I didn't think he would tell. That would be sneaking, and Sir William didn't approve of sneaks.

On a waft of *Quelques Fleurs* our mother was descending the sweeping curved staircase into the hall. She was wearing a long clingy scarlet evening dress and silver sandals.

"Isn't it bath time?" she asked, smiling vaguely at us as if trying to remember who we were. Her fashionably short wavy fair hair shone under the light like a gilded helmet and the skin on her throat was as white and smooth as swan feathers. Our mother was considered to be a beauty, which was one grade below a great beauty, but still meant a steady stream of male visitors at cocktail time with names like Jock and Dizzy and Edward. She was always in an extra specially good mood when Sir William came to stay, which he seemed to be doing a lot lately.

I'd overheard the cook telling Nanny that it was Sir William's important-to-the-war-effort job in steel that was bringing him so often to our part of the world. I knew our father had an equally important and mysterious job in coal. I pictured two enormous figures, one clad in shiny grey metal, the other entirely covered in black coal dust, striding about barking orders at people. Life was full of puzzles and mysteries and things the grown-ups never explained but—unlike today's children—we were not encouraged to ask questions. The grown-ups never listened or answered anyway, and Nanny only ever said useless things like, "Ask no questions, you'll hear no lies."

My mother

"Will you be coming to say goodnight to us?" I asked my mother, always hopeful, although she hardly ever did.

"Not tonight, darling." She skimmed across the flagstone floor, high heels tapping, trailing her scented fingers over our heads as she went by. "Tell the cook dinner will be delayed," she said to Violet, who was holding the drawing room door open for her. "The master won't be home before eight o'clock." The door clicked shut behind her.

"She and Sir William will be quite drunk on gin by the time Daddy gets home," Johnny informed me as we climbed the steep shadowy linoleum-covered nursery stairs.

"Really?" I didn't know what drunk was—or gin for that matter—but I didn't ask. I didn't seem to want to know.

Johnny was home in the middle of the term because his prep school, St Cyprian's, had just burned to the ground in the middle of the night. Johnny had had the distinction of being the last boy out just before the roof caved in, his photo on the front page of all the newspapers. He told me in confidence that he was last because he'd been trying to decide if he could leave his hated school dressing gown behind.

Johnny was three years older than me, and when he wasn't away in the mysterious grey-flannel world of prep school he was my hero, my protector, my tormentor, and the ten-year-old font of all knowledge.

"What's bridge?" I'd asked him one night when we were sitting in the dark at the top of the main staircase long after we were supposed to be asleep, alert for the sound of Nanny's heavy tread. We were listening to the murmur of voices coming from the drawing room where a "bridge party" was in progress.

"Oh, they borrow the tunnels and bridges from my electric train and set them up on the floor and—play bridge," said Johnny. The recent arrival of our brother Thomas had prompted me to ask him if he knew where babies came from. His information on that subject didn't prove to be much more accurate.

I think I'll go back a bit now and tell you how it all started. I know, because when my parents were old and slightly more mellow and approachable, I used to go to stay with them in Cape Town and listen to their stories.

Chapter 2

Blame it on the Black Bottom

My Father

My mother and father met at a Fancy Dress Ball at a terribly grand country house in Yorkshire. The year was 1926, the year the future Queen Elizabeth II was born and Rudolph Valentino died and a Scotsman called James Baird demonstrated a new invention he called television. My future father arrived late at the ball, accompanied by a rowdy group of friends. His stiff white collar was on back-to-front and he was wearing a false nose with attached spectacles. He was supposed to be a vicar.

He came straight up to my mother and said, "May I have this dance?"

"Not unless you take that ridiculous nose off first," said my mother. He did and she said, "Oh well, you might as well put it back on. You looked better before." My father was thirty-seven at the time, handsome as a young

Marlon Brando, spoilt, arrogant, used to having his own way. He had never been married. My mother was twenty-six, vivacious, blonde, divorced, and surely irresistible in her flirty beaded dress.

"Who are you with this evening?" my father asked as he took her in his arms on the dance floor.

"No one," said my mother, "I'm working." She indicated the band leader, suave in white tie and tails and black patent-leather hair. "That's Victor Sylvester. I'm his dancing partner. We teach everyone the new dance steps. This is called the Black Bottom. Do you know how to do it?"

Their whirlwind courtship nearly came to grief the evening my father took my mother home to meet his autocratic old battle-ax of a mother with whom he was still living, rattling about in their vast and hideous ancestral home. The old lady was a widow and only had one son left. She'd lost Cedric to a ruptured appendix and Cyril in the trenches in the First World War. She wasn't interested in her daughters and she certainly wasn't about to relinquish her remaining son without a fight.

"I understand that you are a professional—dancer," she shouted down the dining room table by way of an opening salvo. Dancer was pronounced as if it was synonymous with prostitute.

"Yes, I am," said my mother brightly. A downtrodden little maid crept in to serve the first course.

"And where does this—ah—dancing take place?"

"Oh, we travel all over the country. Luckily my parents take care of Iris for me when I'm away."

"*Iris?*"

"My daughter. She's four. She's so sweet. Eric loves her, don't you, darling?"

The chill in the air must have frozen the not very nice mulligatawny soup. It was the sort of house where curry one night meant mulligatawny soup, (left-over curry put through a sieve), the next.

"Mamma," said my father, "I already told you Margot has a child and that she's divorced."

"*Divorced?*"

If a scarlet A for Adulteress had sprung out on my mother's forehead she couldn't have been more damned. The fact that her husband, known in the family as the Bounder, had run off never to be seen again when she told him she was going to have a baby was no excuse.

But as I mentioned, my father was used to having his own way.

"Where would you like to go on our honeymoon?" he asked his future bride a few weeks later.

"Oh, I don't care," said my besotted mother foolishly, "You decide."

So she spent the first week of her married life fidgeting on a hard bench at Lord's Cricket Ground in London, where a Test Match was in progress. I expect she consoled herself with romantic notions about the second week. She was to be whisked off in my father's terrifying Talbot motor car—all chrome pipes and leather straps over the bonnet which he drove like a maniac—to a fishing village in Cornwall.

Once there, however, she spent the week huddled in a deckchair on a stony, gale-swept beach, anxiously scanning the waves for the triumphant return of

My parents' wedding 1927

her brand new husband with a boat full of dead mackerel. Of course she never changed him.

Imagine my poor mother's dismay when they returned from Cornwall and she realized she was expected to live with her mother-in-law.

"What do we need another house for?" said my father, "what's wrong with this one?"

My parents leaving on their honeymoon

"Darling, this is your mother's house. We need our own house."

"Whatever for? Half the place is closed up and never used. Surely there's more than enough room for everyone?"

"No, darling," said my mother firmly. "There will never be enough room for your mother and me under the same roof. What was that you said? Don't go stamping off. Where are you going?"

"All I said was 'women'. And I'm going to take the dogs for a walk."

But my mother won that round, and she and her little daughter were soon installed a safe distance away in Edwinstowe House in the little mining village of Edwinstowe around which, like an ancient green muffler, lay Robin Hood's fabled Sherwood Forest.

Here they were joined before long by my brother Johnny, and on November 11 three years later my bawling arrival apparently shattered the Two Minute Silence at eleven o'clock on Armistice Day.

Presumably overcome with emotional memories and patriotic fervor, my father suggested I should be called Poppy to honour the day of my birth. Fortunately my mother said she had once known a very nice jersey cow called Poppy, but she would prefer to call her daughter Diana.

No sooner did we arrive with our blue eyes and fair hair than my father turned against poor little green-eyed dark-haired Iris. "I am not your father," he told his step-daughter. "I don't want you to call me Daddy."

So she learned to call him Nunkie instead, and was soon bundled off to boarding school.

My father, whom I was only to get to know towards the end of his life, was a curious mixture of callousness and loyalty, selfishness and generosity. It was typical of him to reject his small step-daughter, but to rescue his sister Betty from their mother's gloomy establishment and have a pretty little bungalow built for

Me and my big brother, Johnny

her in the village. Here he installed her with a nurse and a cook and a maid to take care of her, all of which he paid for.

Betty had developed rheumatoid arthritis when she was eighteen, and by the time I knew her, she was completely paralyzed except for some use of her hands. She was to spend fifty years lying flat on her back—not even a pillow—on a high coach-built black and yellow carriage rather like the landau in which the queen drives down the race course at Ascot, which I suppose my father must have had built specially for her. Unable to move her head, she had an array of mirrors which allowed her to see a little of her limited world. In a shed in Betty's garden lived a vile-tempered donkey called Lassie, who occasionally consented to be harnessed to the carriage so that Betty could be taken for drives and look up at the sky and clouds and trees for a change.

When I was about five, my father started taking me to tea at Betty's bungalow on Sunday afternoons. Off we'd set, my father striding through the village swinging his walking stick, his dogs (and me) trotting at his heels, acknowledging the respectful greetings of miners digging in their gardens or clipping their privet hedges or out strolling with their wives or sweethearts.

My father ran all the coal mines in the district, employed some twelve thousand men and, in my childish eyes at least, cut an awe-inspiring figure of power and splendour. (I should perhaps mention that coal was a vital source of energy at the time, and no one had ever heard of acid rain or greenhouse gasses or global warming.) Having nothing to compare him with, I had no idea that some fathers were different, that they read stories to their children, talked to them, listened to them, got down on the floor and played with them. Such a notion would have been as bizarre as coming across my father waltzing with the cook or balancing the silver cocktail tray on his head.

Tea at the bungalow was served on a card table set up beside Betty's carriage. I was allowed to pour out. Betty sipped her tea through the spout of a special little china tea-pot. She had a white one for tea and another one with pink rosebuds on for her six o'clock cocktail. Unlike in the nursery, you didn't have to finish the bread and butter before you could have a lemon curd tart or a slice of sponge cake or a piece of sticky, treacley flap-jack.

Betty's treasure-trove of a room was so crowded with looming, ornately-carved furniture that you had to be careful edging your way round to look at things. There were Dresden shepherdesses playing with cherubs and gar-lands of flowers or being wooed by men in wigs and knee britches, several deeply interesting bronze statues of both sexes, (interesting because they were naked), and five or six grandfather clocks, all of which chimed at dif-ferent times so you wondered how Betty ever slept at night. The walls were entirely covered with sepia photos and portraits in heavy gilt frames of unknown relatives (unknown because they were mostly dead). Best of all was a glass-topped display table, its interior lined with purple velvet. I had to stand on tip-toe, being careful not to leave finger-prints on the glass, to examine its contents. There were silver trinkets, my father's war medals, intricately carved ivory and jade, a tiny silver hunting horn, a shriveled monkey's paw, a ringlet of dark hair tied with a faded ribbon, a citation for gallantry awarded to Captain Eric Young in the Battle of the Somme, and a telegram regretting to report the death in combat of Major Cyril Young.

After tea, Betty always said, "Eric dear, please lift Diana up here beside me," and my father would swing me up onto the edge of the carriage and go off to inspect the garden.

"Now, lovey," Betty would say, "I want you to tell me *everything* you've been doing this week!"

In a world where no one took much notice of children, this was heaven. Betty's blue eyes sparkled with delight when I told her about luring the leader of village boys' gang into the goose pen, and how the geese had chased him up onto the roof of their shed. Lifting the ruff of dry gray hair away from her ear I whispered, "And do you know what Our-Edly said? He said 'bugger this'!" and Betty laughed till the tears ran down the sides of her face and I had to mop them for her with a corner of the sheet.

Tea at the bungalow was served on a card table
set up beside Betty's carriage

I looked forward to those Sunday tea parties, but soon they were quite spoilt because my father decided it was time to move his increasingly senile mother into the bungalow so that she could be looked after with Betty.

Chapter 3

Two Grannies

My paternal grandmother, Granny Young, had scary hooded eyes like a witch, rheumy and flecked with blood and malice, and long yellow teeth like Lassie the donkey, and she always smelt as if she'd just wet her knickers—which may well have been the case. If I didn't keep my distance, a crusty spider hand would dart out from among her various shawls and cardigans and seize me in a surprisingly powerful grip and she'd breathe her tomb breath in my face and demand, "Aren't you going to give your Granny a kiss?"

Thank goodness my father was there to intervene. "Now Mamma," he'd say, "you know the Queen doesn't go in much for kissing."

How true. My father nicknamed me the Queen after an episode when we were staying in a seaside hotel when I was about four and—horror of horrors—an elderly female guest stopped me at the foot of the stairs as Nanny was taking me up to bed and said, "Dear little girl, may I kiss you goodnight?"

"No," I said. Then, seeing Nanny's frown, I extended my hand over the banister and said, "but you may kiss my hand if you like."

I was a terribly smell-conscious little girl. I dreaded occasional trips to Mansfield or Nottingham with my mother to buy me new shoes because of the crowded pavements and the way peoples' coats and trouser legs brushed against me. They smelt disgustingly of dirty dusters and pigs' trotters and the inside of the pigeon cote. I held my breath as much as possible, and often became quite blue in the face if we had far to go. Another thing was that my mother sometimes left me alone in the car while she "just ran into" some shop and I was convinced she was never coming back. *Child Found Starved To Death In Car.* To this day I'd rather have a root canal than go shopping.

The only thing I did quite like about shoe-shopping was peering down into the X-ray machine and watching my toes wiggle inside my new shoes. Sometimes Johnny came with us for new shoes too, and he and I kept pressing the button and taking it in turns to look at our own and each others' toes. Children must have been exposed to shocking amounts of x-ray in shoe shops in those days, apparently with no serious consequences.

I loved my other grandmother as much as I loathed Granny Young. When Grandpa and Granny Hayward came to stay at Edwinstowe, a highlight of their visit came at bedtime each evening when my grandmother would appear at the night nursery door and say, "Good evening, Nanny. May I borrow Diana's nimble fingers?"

She always wore her mass of snowy hair coiled on the top of her head like a crown which seemed too heavy for her frail neck, and her wrinkled fingers and wrists, which were almost as small as mine, were weighed down with old-fashioned pearl and ruby rings and gold bracelets. Across the blue linoleum she'd skim and alight on the edge of my bed like a tiny jewel-bright humming bird, and I'd inhale the lovely scent of rose geranium soap and Yardley's Lavender Water. Kneeling behind her, proud of my important task, I'd fasten the difficult little fabric-covered buttons and loops all the way up the back of one of her identical high-necked long-sleeved crimson or purple or emerald velvet evening dresses. If you got one button wrong you had to begin all over again. Sometimes I got one wrong on purpose so I could keep her sitting on my bed a bit longer.

Because of her addiction to the telephone, my father had nick-named my maternal grandmother Mrs. Bell after its inventor. This became Ting-a-Ling and eventually Ting.

High-spirited Ting was an unlikely wife for a quiet, scholarly country vicar. Church services frankly bored her, and she would drop her prayer book and tap her foot if Grandfather's sermon ran over its allotted ten minutes. She timed him on his own gold watch, laid before her on the pew in full view of the rest of the congregation.

They lived in an enormous, dilapidated, wind-battered *Wuthering Heights*-type rectory in Yorkshire, and had somehow managed to raise and educate five children on Grandfather's stipend of four hundred pounds a year. My beautiful mother claimed to have been the ugly duckling of that handsome and flamboyant flock. Her father called her 'Bappy', and when she was little he always had her to sit next to him at meals to protect her from her three brothers' teasing.

"Leave some bread and butter for Bappy."

"Pass Bappy the sugar. No, Pascoe, that's the salt."

Pascoe, the eldest, was destined to become a highly respected barrister and King's Council, and you had to feel sorry for any criminal unfortunate enough to land in his court. Just one look from beneath those shaggy eyebrows was certainly enough to quell the most unruly child.

One drowsy summer afternoon when Uncle Pascoe was sleeping off the effects of Sunday lunch in the garden at Edwinstowe, on a dare from my brother Johnny, (who, I might add, remained safely hidden in the rhododendron bushes), I crept across the lawn to tie the end of a piece of rope to the back of his deckchair. The idea was that a sudden jerk of the rope would collapse the chair, and Pascoe's awesome dignity with it.

Unfortunately for our plan, he wasn't as sound asleep as we thought. As I was fumbling with the knot, a hand suddenly reached round and seized me and I found myself trapped between a pair of scratchy tweed knees, my face only inches away from that alarming countenance.

"Little girl," rumbled Pascoe in his deep voice, "if you ever do anything like that again I shall cut you up in small pieces and put you in a sack and throw you in the swimming pool and no one will ever know what became of you."

Poor Pascoe. He was actually quite fond of us children and I'm sure it never occurred to him that I didn't realize he was teasing me. He must have wondered why I avoided being alone with him for a long time after the deckchair incident.

My mother told me that when she was a child she loved to accompany her father on parish visits, clip-clopping along between the hedgerows in a high-wheeled gig drawn by a dappled grey horse.

On one occasion her father took her to say goodbye to their old gardener, who was not long for this world. They found him lying on a truckle bed in a corner of the tiny cottage kitchen, its window fogged with steam from a ham boiling away in a big black pot. The old fellow raised himself shakily on his elbow to greet them. Then, sniffing the air, he said to his wife, "Ee, lass, I could just do with a bit of that there 'am."

"Ney, lad," she replied briskly, "thee can't 'ave none of that. 'Tis for the funeral."

Before dealers and American tourists sent prices spiraling out of sight, Granny Ting collected antiques. One day she spied a cupboard standing out in the rain in a muddy farm yard, slapped over with white paint and being used to store tools and harness.

"If I get you a new cupboard, may I have that one?" she asked the puzzled farmer.

Her quick eye had recognized a priceless seventeenth century court cupboard, (once used to store some nobleman's Court robes), and she had it home and restored to its former glory before Grandpa could say, "Now, Ethel, my dear, you know we can't afford—."

Ting eventually gave the court cupboard to my parents as a wedding present and it stood in the hall at Edwinstowe, crammed with coats and Wellington boots and walking sticks and riding crops, a popular hiding place in games of hide-and-seek.

One of the last times I saw Ting she was in hospital, recovering from a small operation. She was in her late eighties by then, and had been a widow for many years. I was eighteen and newly married. A flustered young nurse carrying a dustpan and brush met me outside her room. "She asked to borrow my scissors!" the poor girl wailed, "I'm so sorry, but how was I to know she'd do anything so terrible?"

I found Ting sitting up in bed looking like a naughty angel, her small head wreathed in curls. She had cut off all her beautiful hair. Long silvery hanks lay scattered on the floor round her bed.

"Ting! Your hair! Why?"

"They won't let me get up," said Ting. "I was bored."

The nurse swept up the hair and removed the scissors and departed. Glancing round, I saw that the room was a bower of flowers.

"Heavens, Ting," I said, laying my small offering of freesias on the bed, "you've got a flower shop in here! Where did all these come from?"

"Oh," she said evasively, "just some foolish young man. Now, tell me about your honeymoon. How was Madeira?"

As the young say nowadays, I wasn't about to "go there." I was never going to tell a soul about lying awake beside my sleeping husband in the luxurious bridal suite of Reed's Hotel, listening to the shush-shush of the ocean, watching the moonlight move across the floor, feeling rather sore, and wondering, "Could the Duke of Windsor really have given up the throne of England for *this*?"

Ting's 'foolish young man,' she finally admitted, was the vicar of a nearby parish. He was in his seventies. He'd been asking her to marry him for years but she always turned him down. In my frame of mind at the time, I couldn't say I blamed her.

Ting must have had strong genes. One of my daughters, whose name happens to be Ming, has inherited her heavy ropes of silky hair, her sapphire eyes, and the same engaging way of wrinkling her finely chiseled nose when she laughs.

Looking at a photo on my desk of Ming's little daughter, it's clear that those same genes have traveled from the wilds of Yorkshire and turned up again in Ting's great, great, granddaughter Serena, who is growing up on the Hawaiian island of Maui.

Chapter 4

The Big House

Edwinstowe House, generally referred to by the locals simply as the big 'ouse, lay at the edge of the old village of Edwinstowe, its acres of formal gardens surrounded by a high red brick wall on two sides and a flood dyke and a small river on the other two.

Edwinstowe House 1940

The adjacent new village, my father's pride and joy, was where most of the miners and their families lived in row upon row of identical red brick semi-detached houses. Each house had its own narrow strip of garden, where the miners grew vegetables and raised rabbits for the pot and homing pigeons for racing, and where their wives pegged out their washing on Mondays.

Unlike the terrible Orwellian conditions in which coal miners had lived in the quite recent past, each of the houses in this new "model" village had hot and cold running water, a bathroom and indoor lavatory and, contrary to the predictions of those opposed to its construction, (mainly the owners of the coal mines), the miners did not keep coal in their bathtubs.

My father was also having pithead baths and lockers built at all the mines in his charge so the men didn't have to trudge home in their filthy clothes, black from head to foot with coal dust. Later he would also go to America and buy modern coal-cutting machinery, which meant that the miners no longer had to crouch and hack at the coal face with pickaxes and load it into pony-drawn wagons with shovels.

But even with these improvements, mining remained a filthy, dangerous, health-destroying job, and from time to time the pithead siren would still shriek out its dreaded warning of an accident underground. When this spine-chilling sound ripped through the village the women would burst from their houses like flocks of startled starlings, still in their aprons and curlers, and run through the village towards the mine with terror-stricken faces, each praying it wouldn't be one of their own trapped or crushed or mangled far below our feet.

Perhaps it was the very danger of the miners' jobs which bound the community so closely, and an unspoken pride in hazardous work well done that made generations of sons follow their fathers and grandfathers down into the mines. Or perhaps it was simply a lack of any alternative. Whatever the truth may be, (a bit of both, probably), the community spirit was tangible and real—and something that is vanishing from much of our modern world.

You approached our house between tall, mossy, red brick columns surmounted by big grey stone balls flanking a white-painted gate which always stood open. The curving granite-chip drive was edged by wide grass verges and flowerbeds bright in summer with a dense jungle of shaggy-headed dahlias. They were taller than I was and crawling with earwigs which Johnny and I used to collect in matchboxes, planning to put them in visitors' beds, though I don't think we ever did.

Every Saturday I woke to the rattling sound made by Fairfax the head gardener dragging a piece of matting with wooden strips of nails under-neath—a sort of inverted Fakir's bed—up and down the drive. On Saturday mornings the drive, free of hoof and tire marks, flowed down to the entrance gates like an old man's well-combed grey beard.

The house dated from the seventeenth century and had a grey slate roof and tall cream-painted sash windows and a stone mounting-block by the front door. Its mellow red brick walls were thickly clad with Virginia creeper and dusty, bitter-scented ivy which rustled with quarrelsome spar-rows and was home to still more earwigs. Johnny said the earwigs were going to come swarming over the night nursery window-sill some night, march across the floor, up the bed leg, straight into my ears and eat my brain while I was asleep. It never occurred to me to ask why he wasn't wor-ried about them eating *his* brain. Johnny also invented "The Man Who Pokes You in the Back."

"The Man who Pokes You in the Back is here," a ghoul whisper would come out of the darkness just as I was falling asleep, and he'd lean out of his bed and jab his finger in my back. Frightened out of my wits, I'd bur-row to the foot of my bed—only to wake in the night suffocating in a tan-gle of sheets and blankets and grope frantically round the wrong end of the bed for the bedside light—which of course wasn't there.

"Well," said Nanny in the morning, "I never knew anyone make such a dog's dinner of their bed. Just look how tidy your brother's bed is."

You almost needed a passport to cross the frontiers dividing Edwinstowe House. Children lived under the benign dictatorship of Nanny in the nursery and the servants had their quarters in the Third World behind the green baize door. Our parents and their visitors and friends naturally saw little reason to leave their part of the house and travel to those remote and relatively primitive regions.

The nursery had its own staircase up which coal scuttles had to be carried several times a day in winter and all our meals brought up on trays from the distant kitchens. A typical nursery lunch consisted of minced

meat stewed in gravy, boiled cabbage and mashed potatoes, followed by rice pudding. There was water to drink. Plain food was considered to be good for children—and probably was. In any case junk food and sweet fizzy drinks in cans had yet to be invented.

The day nursery had a wide arched window whose lower half was barred to prevent us climbing out and falling through the glass roof of the conservatory below. There was an oval oak table which had seen better days under the window where we had our meals and did our lessons, and a fireplace with a high green mesh fender with a polished brass rail where our

Nanny and her charges

pajamas were put to warm at bedtime. Before the fire lay a woolly blue hearth-rug. Hand-hooked by Nanny, it depicted a cheerful row of marching teddy bears. Our toy cupboards flanked the fireplace, and there was a bookcase and a wind-up gramophone with some blunt needles and few smeary *His Master's Voice* records: *The Teddy Bears' Picnic*. Stanley Holloway singing *Sam, Sam, Pick Up Thee Musket and Scram*. For a time

Johnny was so addicted to this record that our father eventually began calling him Sam, a name that stuck long after the craze had passed.

The loose cover of Nanny's armchair beside the fire had worn and split along the outsides of the arms, making deep pockets where marbles or missing bits of jigsaw or lead soldiers or plates of dolls' house food sometimes mysteriously turned up. The faded fabric was printed with fox-hunting scenes and matched the curtains till Johnny accidentally set them on fire with his mentholated-spirit-driven steam engine.

Television still lay several years in the future, but we were allowed to listen to *The Children's Hour* every weekday evening between five and six o'clock on the nursery wireless. "Uncle Mac" read us stories, and there were the serialized adventures of *Tarzan* and *Robinson Crusoe* and *Toad of Toad Hall* and *Larry the Lamb*, who lived in Toy-Town.

Our entertainment was certainly a far cry from that of today's children, who are barely expected to go on a journey in the car without a DVD player mounted in the back.

I sometimes wonder, observing modern children's tightly structured and scheduled lives and electronic toys and access to round-the-clock entertainment, when there is time for their imagination to develop—something that needs a degree of solitude and even boredom. What child today would, (or would be allowed to), spend a wet afternoon watching two raindrops stopping and starting down a window pane, inventing adventures for them, giving them names, urging one or the other to get to the bottom of the pane first? Or fritter away a summer afternoon lying in the grass, hands cupped on either side of her face, enthralled by the drama of a busy miniature world; a beetle hurrying by on an urgent mission, an ant's persistence in pushing and pulling something ten times its size through the green jungle, the tight-rope skills of a tiny insect balanced on a blade of grass?

In our early years, Johnny and I shared a night nursery at Edwinstowe. It was furnished with two blue-painted wooden beds, two blue bedside tables and two blue chests of drawers. A small and ineffectual coal fire provided the only heat, and two windows faced each other across an expanse of cracked blue linoleum. In the middle of the ceiling hung an opaque white globe held in four metal claws. I hated that light. I imagined it was a blind world held in the clutches of some malevolent bird and I was careful never to be looking at it when Nanny switched it off at bedtime. It gave me bad dreams.

Very occasionally our father, resplendent in his dinner jacket, would startle us by striding into the night nursery at bed time. He didn't come to kiss his sweet little blond-haired children goodnight. He came, much to Nanny's silent disapproval, to make sure that the top buttons of our pajama jackets were left un-fastened, and that both the windows were wide open—regardless of the weather. He abhorred what he called "Fug rats."

Sometimes when we woke on winter mornings, snow had drifted across the floor. On windy nights the thin, washed-out cotton curtains on one side of the room rose up and flapped against the ceiling like ghosts and on the other they streamed and snapped out into the howling blackness as if struggling to wrench themselves free and fly away.

A cavernous claw-footed bath tub stood in the middle of the nursery bathroom, its chipped enamel shower hood reaching up to the ceiling. Filled to the brim, the bath was big enough and deep enough to swim in (if you knew how).

When war-time restrictions caused a red line to be painted near the plug, rationing us to five inches of water, we invented a new game. After our baths we let out the water and rubbed the inside of the bath with soap. Then we took it in turns to sit on the edge at one end and slide at great speed down the slippery slope and along the bottom of the bath to the plug end, push off with our feet and slide back even faster. Johnny got going at such speed once that he shot right out of the bath, flew across the bathroom, and crashed into the fat behind of Joan the nursery maid, who leaning over the wash basin, engaged in her everlasting task of squeezing blackheads out of her nose in the mirror.

"Can't you watch where you're going?" said Joan, and went on squeezing.

Our lavatory was in a long narrow room next door. The lavatory itself was a massive throne-like mahogany structure of such height and width and depth that that I had to hold on so I didn't fall in and my legs stuck straight out when I was sent to sit there "till I'd done something" every morning after breakfast.

Most days Nanny sent us, dressed according to the weather, out into the garden to play, which was fine with us. Come rain or shine there was always plenty to do. For instance, we could try to slip into the conservatory and steal a few grapes or a nectarine when Parker's back was turned. He was the dear, grumpy, almost blind old gardener whose specialty was growing such exotic (for Nottinghamshire) fruit. He also grew mushrooms in a dank, dark, malodorous shed we were fairly sure was haunted and, apparently to please my father, carnations in every imaginable horrid clashing colour in a special greenhouse devoted to nothing else. He disapproved of us sitting on the wet grass because we'd get what he called "the screwmatics" (rheumatism) like him.

When none of the other gardeners were about, there were raspberries and strawberries and sweet young peas and carrots in their season to steal from the kitchen garden, and Johnny sometimes took pigeon eggs from the fantail pigeons' dove-cote beneath the copper beech tree. He cooked them in a little tin pan on the wobbly—and I should think terribly dangerous—primus stove in our Wendy house, and ate them with much ostentatious lip-smacking because he knew it made me feel sick.

In summer I ran a hospital on a sun-warmed slab of stone beside the swimming pool. My patients were the insects and butterflies I fished out of the water with a butterfly net. I loved to watch them revive and begin to groom their legs and antennas and move their tiny wings and eventually crawl or fly away. In the holidays I had to guard my hospital from Johnny's less altruistic attentions.

There was also nearly always something interesting going on in the stable yard. There were our father's gun dogs to talk to through the wire net-ting of their run, or Cartledge the groom to watch mucking out the stables or feeding the horses or cleaning their tack with lovely smelling saddle soap. A steady procession of delivery boys came to the kitchen door with fish or meat or bread covered in white cloths in the big baskets on the handlebars of their bicycles, and sometimes Arthur drove into the yard with a great clatter of hooves and a lot of shouts of "Whoa there!" and "Get oop!" at his huge horse, come to deliver a cart-load of coal in big greasy black sacks. The interesting thing about Arthur was that when he smiled, which he did a lot, you saw that his teeth were as black as his coal.

Sometimes dark-eyed gypsy women with gold hoops in their ears and ragged clothes and babies wrapped in shawls came to the kitchen door carrying baskets of hand-made wooden clothes pegs for sale, or small sprigs of "lucky" white heather, or an offer to read the tea-leaves in the maids' tea cups. Fascinated though we were, we didn't approach the gypsies too closely. Rumour had it that they sometimes stole children. *Gone with the raggle-taggle gypsies oh!* as the song warned, never to be seen again.

When Johnny was home from school we spent a lot of time building

Never allowed to bat

dens, climbing trees, doing battle with the village boys, playing cricket, (I was hardly ever allowed to bat), and cowboys and Indians, (I always had to be the Indian, left tied to a tree sometimes till darkness began to fall), and, of course, Robin Hood and Maid Marion.

We also spent endless hours trying to catch sparrows with a trap made from a dustbin lid propped on a stick with a length of string tied to it. When a bold sparrow hopped under the lid to peck at the bread-crumb bait you jerked the string from your hiding place and down crashed the dustbin lid. We never actually caught a sparrow, but that didn't seem to matter.

Alone in the garden when Johnny was away, I made scent for the maids from rose petals soaked for a long time in water, which turned a rather disappointing brownish colour and didn't smell very nice, but it was always received with cries of delight. I also collected the rust-coloured seeds of sorrel weeds, which resembled the tobacco Fred the under-gardener smoked in his pipe. I filled his discarded tobacco tins with the stuff and sold them back to kind Fred for a farthing (four farthings made a penny).

I also had a stable of hobby horses which kept me busy. Made from my father's old socks tied to sticks, their bridles made of string, to me they were as real as the real horses; the black was a handful, but a good jumper, the grey was nervous and shied a lot, the brown was placid and easy-going. Fairfax let me stable them in his potting shed with flower pots for their food and water.

When the weather confined me indoors, an absorbing solitary occupation involved a family of marbles, all with names and personalities, who lived and had adventures in hills and caves fashioned from an old discarded bath-mat.

Monday was Wash Day, and at dawn a fire was lit under the big "copper" in the stone-floored wash-house next to the saddle room in the stable yard. Here the sheets and towels and our clothes and the maids' uniforms were boiled in great rolling clouds of steam and pummeled with a wooden implement softened and bleached by immersion in hot water called a dolly. The dolly consisted of a long stick with a handle at one end and a disk with four thick wooden pegs at the other that looked rather like a cow's udder. When not in use, it stood behind the wash-house door and made quite a satisfactory sort of pogo stick. Something called a Blue Bag (probably because that's what they were; small muslin bags full of blue powder) was added to the whites to make them whiter. A dampened Blue Bag was also rubbed on wasp stings and insect bites to take the pain away. It didn't work very well.

After a copper-full of laundry had been boiled and beaten to within an inch of its life, everything was lifted out of the boiling water with big wooden tongs and dropped into huge galvanized metal tubs of clean water to be rinsed twice then, with much grunting and heaving, passed through a hand-operated mangle.

After that everything had to be carried in big wicker baskets to the clothes lines in the kitchen garden and pegged out to dry, the clothes-lines pushed high into the wind with heavy wooden clothes-props. With luck, (a lot of luck given the English climate), the rain would hold off and everything would be dry by the end of the day, and could be taken down from the clothes lines and carried into the laundry room ready for Ironing Day on Tuesday.

Wash Day took up the entire day, and involved a huge amount of heavy physical labour. You can't help wondering what the exhausted washerwoman and her harassed little assistant would have said at the end of a Monday Wash Day if you could have shown them today's gleaming white automatic washers and driers.

After tea on most afternoons when we were small Nanny delivered us, scrubbed and changed into clean clothes, to the drawing room to spend half an hour with our mother and any friends she happened to be entertaining. I suppose we made a pretty enough picture, leaning against her armchair, blinking in the cigarette smoke, the laughter and chatter swirling incomprehensibly round our well-brushed heads. But I'm afraid it must be said that we shared our mother's evident relief when Nanny arrived to remove us.

The drawing room suffered for a while from one of my mother's periodic decorating brain-storms. Probably under the influence of some modern 30s fad for tubular steel and plate glass furniture and pale wood, out went all the lovely old antique furniture and squashy chintz sofas and chairs, and in came uncomfortable tubular steel furniture upholstered in bilious green tweed, several limed-oak occasional tables the dogs kept knocking over, and a black glass drinks table supported by what looked like scaffolding. The old Dutch painting over the fireplace was replaced with a Cezanne reproduction, and a nasty black glass clock and a souvenir imitation-bronze copy of *Resting Achilles* appeared on the mantelpiece. I don't know what my father must have thought of this hideous transformation, but luckily the old furniture had only been banished to a storeroom, and was reinstated when my mother recovered.

Next to the drawing room was our father's study with its collection of polished brass shell cases clustered by the fire. Like the blue shadows of shrapnel still in his legs and clearly visible when he wore his bathing suit, the shell cases were souvenirs from The Great War. It was my least favourite room in the house because Nanny occasionally sent one of us there to be punished for some crime of such naughtiness as to be beyond the scope of her discipline. I can't imagine what those crimes could have been, or what punishment we received, but if Johnny was ever beaten he never said, and my father certainly never spanked or even smacked me. Still, those dreaded trips to the study must have started when I was quite small because I have a clear recollection of standing outside the door, trying to pluck up the courage to knock, and being fascinated by the distorted reflection of my face—which was exactly level with the polished oval brass doorknob. Once I became so engrossed in pulling faces at myself that I must have forgotten why I was there, and after a bit I trotted off, unpunished, and returned to the nursery.

Across the hall from the drawing room was the billiards room, whose brown velvet curtains held the pungent scent of cigar smoke and from where some nights could be heard loud male voices and shouts of laughter. I quite liked the smell of the curtains and the pretty coloured balls on the green baize table, but I avoided the room because of all the poor dead stuffed animals on the walls and standing around in glass cases. They included pheasants and partridges and grouse frozen in eternal flight, grinning foxes' masks and foxes' bushy white-tipped brushes, a stag's head, a sweet owl, and a terrified-looking hare in mid-leap.

At the end of the hall was the dining room, which glowed with Sheraton and Chippendale furniture and the muted reds of an old Turkish carpet. The sideboard sparkled with beautifully polished silver mugs and candelabra and engraved salvers and cigarette boxes. In one of its sides was a discrete little cupboard where, before the advent of modern plumbing, a chamber-pot had been kept for the use of male guests after the ladies had withdrawn and left them to their port.

My godfather Filson

Over the sideboard hung a gloomy oil painting of battleships in line astern in tumultuous seas painted by my father's cousin, my infamous godfather Filson Young, whose name I was given at my christening. Unfortunately I never knew my godfather because my father threw him out of the house for trying to seduce my mother when I was still a baby. As I don't look in the least like my brothers, and have grown up to be a writer and artist like Filson, I've naturally wondered if he might not have had more success with his dastardly designs on my mother's virtue some nine months or so earlier.

Recent research on the Internet revealed that Filson published countless books in his lifetime, one of which is still regarded as a definitive history of the early motor car and its impact on society. (I wonder what he'd have to say about its impact today.) Another, about the sinking of the *Titanic*, was rushed into print within a month of the disaster, and one of his novels had the distinction of being burned in Scotland due to its salacious content. Filson was also a war correspondent, (I found a photo of him on a horse at the Relief of Mafeking in the Boer War), poet, world traveler, raconteur, womanizer and voluminous letter-writer. In other words, the sort of man you'd give anything to sit next to at dinner.

His only son, my wild, handsome, fair-haired cousin (or half-brother?) Billy gave me a little jade monkey on a chain and told me he was going to marry me when I grew up. But Billy was never to see his nineteenth birthday. He crashed into the English Channel in an exploding ball of fire when his fighter plane was shot down during the Battle of Britain.

A typical Filson anecdote quoted on the Internet concerns an incident when he was doing some research in the Royal Library at Windsor Castle when King George V walked in.

"Who the devil are you?" demanded the King.

"Filson Young," replied my godfather coolly, "who are you?"

Given the violent nature of Filson's expulsion from our lives, I've wondered why my father continued to keep his painting over the sideboard in the dining room.

All through the war, and even on the rare occasions when they dined alone, my parents changed for dinner every night. My mother always wore a long evening dress and my father put on his dinner jacket and the table

Filson's son, my cousin
(or half-brother?) Billy

was elaborately laid with silver and crystal, flowers, lace mats, candles and white damask table napkins.

My mother called it, "Not letting one's standards slip just because there's a war on."

"Isn't Margot wonderful?" said her friends admiringly.

They always had three courses and they were waited on by Ivy, summoned by a bell under the carpet beside my mother's foot. The only exception to all this rigmarole was on Sundays, when most of the servants were given the evening off. My parents didn't change, and they and made do with scrambled eggs and helped themselves from the hotplate.

"No wonder Margot's servants never leave," her friends often remarked, "she's so good to them."

All throught the war and even on the rare occassion when
they dined alone, my parents changed for dinner every evening

Chapter 5

Rare Events

Apart from Christmas Day, the only meal we children had in the dining room with our parents was Sunday lunch, and a very mixed blessing it was too. For one thing, you had to eat everything on your plate—which included blood-oozing roast beef or roast leg of lamb and mint sauce or pork with disgusting greasy crackling.

Living as I did in the world of Beatrix Potter and Alison Utley and Little Grey Rabbit going to market with her bonnet and shopping basket, I had become a vegetarian at an early age. Seated across the wide mahogany table from me at Sunday lunch, Johnny would wait till he caught my eye and then cram the forkful of trembling yellow beef fat he'd been saving into his mouth, almost making me be sick on the spot.

If my father saw me trying to hide a piece of meat under my knife and fork he would throw his napkin down on the table and get up and stride through the communi-

Me with my hero and tormentor, Johnny

cating door into his study to telephone Mrs. Skafe. Mrs. Skafe was a witch who lived in Mansfield Woodhouse. Naughty little girls could be sent to live with her and be fed on mud pies if they didn't eat their Sunday lunch.

"Hello, Mrs. Skafe," I'd hear him say, and my heart would begin to thud and my armpits prickle and I'd somehow choke down the piece of meat. Naturally I didn't know you could depress the bar on the telephone and pretend to have a conversation.

Eventually I devised a hamster-like method of packing the meat into my cheeks and keeping it there till I could escape and spit it out. This rather spoilt the only good part of Sunday lunch, which was being allowed to get down from your chair and go to the sideboard and choose from an array of different puddings. There would be trifle, fruit salad, jelly, treacle tart, apple and plum and lemon meringue pies, and sometimes a chocolate blancmange rabbit with whipped cream for a tail. All very difficult to enjoy with your cheeks stuffed with meat.

Later, as wartime rationing took effect, meals became simpler, but the vegetarian battle raged on.

"You'll never grow up to be a big strong girl if you don't eat your meat," said Nanny.

Wrong, Nanny dear. I grew up to be nearly six feet tall and as strong as a horse. If I'd eaten meat I'd probably have been eight foot tall and ended up in a circus freak show with the bearded woman.

Opening off the wide landing at the top of the main staircase was my parents' bedroom. If I happened to be passing in the evening and their door was ajar and my mother, seated at her dressing table, caught sight of me in the mirror she'd sometimes call, "Darling! Come and talk to me while I'm doing my face."

The room was warm and softly lit and smelt deliciously of my mother's peachy scent. My mother would already have changed into one of her evening dresses. There'd be tiny high-heeled shoes scattered about the floor and discarded clothes flung everywhere, (Violet the housemaid's job to put them away), and from open drawers spilled drifts of delicate pastel-coloured silk and satin and lacey underwear. On the glass-topped dressing table stood clusters of crystal bottles, a jewel case straight from Aladdin's cave, silver-framed photos, and a set of brushes and combs and a hand mirror backed with blue enamel which matched my mother's eyes.

After a little silence she'd usually say something like, "So what have you been doing today?" and I'd reply, "Oh, playing," and we'd smile rather shyly at each other. We didn't really have much to talk about, having so little idea of each other's lives. But I was thrilled just to be standing beside her and watching as she turned her head from side to side, studying her reflection, fiddling with her hair, dabbing a little more Coty's powder on her face with a swan's-down powder puff. Sometimes she'd meet my eyes in the mirror and turn on her tapestry-covered stool and dab my nose too. Such moments made my heart sing.

"Run along now, darling," she'd say, and I'd skip off in a trance of happiness.

My father's dressing room next door was dull by comparison, though I quite liked the other-worldly smell of his clothes. I also liked the chestnut and ebony shine of his shoes, the scratchiness of tweed, the moleskin feel of velvet, the glossy new moon made by a pile of the stiff white collars he attached to his shirts with special studs. His clothes, looked after by Herbert the chauffeur, were kept in a special big wardrobe called a compactum, the shelves and drawers lined with sweet-smelling cedar, each with its small ivory label: *Shirts, Pajamas, Socks.*

Compared with today's candle-lit designer extravaganzas, my parents' bathroom was Spartan in the extreme; white tiles, a black and white checked floor, and plain white free-standing fixtures—which oddly enough seem to have had a fashion revival recently.

On Saturday mornings, if I could dodge Nanny, I would join my father's favourite gun dog—a back spaniel called Dinky—outside their bathroom door.

Dinky always seemed to know when it was Saturday. Saturday was shooting day.

I tried hard not to think about it being last day in the lives of countless pheasants and partridges who, by nightfall, would be hanging by their poor little scaly feet in the cellar with blood dripping from their beaks.

Dinky didn't share my feelings. On the contrary, he was trembling with joyful anticipation.

If we were in luck, my father would open the bathroom door and invite us in to watch him shave. As he used a cutthroat razor which he sharpened on a leather strap hanging beside the basin, this performance was not without drama. When he'd finished shaving he'd wash out the chipped enamel mug, (another souvenir from The Great War). he used for rinsing his shaving brush and fill it with water and say to Dinky, "Want a drink then, old chap?"

Dinky would jump about and bark with exaggerated enthusiasm, then he'd drink, his curly black ears spread on the black and white floor on either side of the mug.

I loved being allowed to share those moments of intimacy between my father and his beloved dog.

The servants' part of the house was officially out of bounds to us children, which naturally gave it the allure of Bluebeard's locked room.

Me with Violet and Ivy

Ivy the parlourmaid and Violet the housemaid were both present throughout our childhood and, busy though they were from morning till night, they loved us and were always pleased to see us. Most of the cooks we had, (who for some reason never seemed to stay long), were less friendly. They shared a common aversion to "children under their feet," and made it clear we were not welcome in their kitchens.

I never ventured into the butler's pantry again after the time I dropped in to watch the silver being polished, (pink Goddard's Plate Powder mixed with mentholated spirits), and surprised the new butler finishing off the dregs in the port decanter. Caught in the act, he leapt across the pantry like "The great, long, red-legged scissor-man." and seized me by the arm and dragged me over to the open door of the silver vault—a cave-like little green baize-lined room with a door as thick and heavy as a submarine's—and hissed in my ear, "If you mention what you just saw I'll lock you in the vault and you'll never be 'eard of again."

Luckily he didn't last long.

"Here," said Johnny, home from school for the holidays, "dare you to put this in Ivy or Violet's bed." From behind his back he produced the tail of the pig which had been slaughtered that day at Home Farm. It had just been delivered, hacked into pieces and wrapped in blood-stained cloths in wicker laundry baskets like aristocrats' heads from the *guillotine* in the French Revolution.

The men had taken the baskets into the larder where they tipped the whole horrible bloody mess into the big stone sink which stood in the middle of the floor. Eventually the meat would be salted, smoked, turned into sausages and pork-pies and otherwise preserved and the fat rendered down in a great blackened cauldron. Nothing would be wasted. The whole thing made me feel sick. Besides, I was fond of the pigs, the way they loved having their bristly backs scratched with a stick, their sweet ears, their clever little eyes. It wasn't their fault they were dirty and smelly. Who wouldn't be, having to live in those disgusting sties?

But I never could resist a dare from Johnny. I took the pig's tail with shrinking fingers. Its skin felt distressingly human. Was it still—warm?

The end where it had been joined to the pig was moist and oozing watery pink blood.

It was the first time I'd ever ventured up the forbidden staircase leading to the maids' bedrooms. They were steep and almost pitch dark and the air was stale and musty and smelt of mice. I emerged into the faint light falling across a passage from a high-up window festooned with spider webs.

Opening the first door I came to, I saw Ivy's best brown coat and hat hanging on a hook on the wall. The only sound was the ticking of a big round alarm clock on the window-sill, which was speckled with dead flies. Three iron beds stood in a row beneath the window, which had no curtains. Three small chests of drawers were lined up along the opposite wall. Their paint was chipped and scratched and some of the drawer handles were missing. The floor was splintery wooden planks. A naked bulb hung from the middle of the ceiling. It was terribly cold. On one of the beds lay a limp pink satin nightdress case with 'Violet' loopily stitched across it. There were little mauve violets embroidered round the name, puckering the shiny fabric. I couldn't have said why, but it was the saddest thing I'd ever seen.

Had my parents ever *been* to this part of the house? Surely if they had they'd do something about the bare bulb, the thin grey bedding, the splintery floor, the freezing temperature? Maybe Sir William should have been lecturing them, not us, about the responsibilities of the privileged to those less fortunate than themselves.

Suddenly our prank didn't seem very funny any more. I opened the window and sent the pig's tail sailing out into the rain. It landed among the last of the cabbages and Brussels sprouts and knotted onion tops in the kitchen garden.

I scurried back down the dark stairs and returned thoughtfully to the warmth of the nursery fire.

In the afternoons, having spent the mornings scrubbing and polishing and doing housework and being interrupted by ringing bells and the telephone to answer, Ivy and Violet had baths and changed out of their gray and white striped dresses and starched white aprons into black georgette dresses, faded to grey in the armpits, and frilly organdy caps and aprons.

After they'd served and cleared away drawing room tea and nursery tea and taken the cocktail tray to the drawing room, their evening duties included curtains to be drawn, beds to be turned down, pajamas and nightdresses to be laid out, dinner to be served and cleared away and washed up. Later, rubber hot water bottles would be slid between elegantly monogrammed but icily cold linen sheets.

Their days started at dawn and seldom finished before ten o'clock and they had one half-day off a week and every other Sunday after tea. I think they were paid about twenty pounds a year.

When I was older, and allowed to stay up a little later, I was sometimes in the drawing room when the grandfather clock in the hall chimed eight o'clock and Ivy appeared at the door to announce: "Dinner is served, Madam."

If she was a few minutes late my mother would glance at the clock on the mantelpiece and sigh and say bravely, "Well, what can one expect with a war on?"

All but one of the coal mines which sustained the village when we lived there have been closed for many years now.

Researching this book, I read on the Internet that Edwinstowe House had recently been restored from the semi-derelict condition into which it had fallen and turned into a centre for high-tech start-up companies in the Midlands.

Reading on, I learned that the opening ceremony had been attended by "one of the oldest residents in the village, who remembers being in domestic service in the house during The Second World War." I scrolled down— and there on the screen appeared a photograph of our housemaid, Violet, with a saucy 40s hat perched over one eye!

Of course I wrote to her at once, re-establishing a contact which had been broken some fifty years previously.

A few years, later on a trip over from the States where I live now with my second husband, we went up to Edwinstowe to have tea with Violet. She was in her late eighties by then, a widow, living in a neat little cottage in the village. We were entertained with home-made scones and flap-jack for tea—and hilarious tales of the youthful high-jinks she and Ivy got up to during the war with the soldiers from the military camp. Her old eyes twinkling with remembered mischief, she told us of nocturnal escapades which would have scandalized my parents—had they not been tucked up and sound asleep between their linen sheets at the time.

"Ivy and me, we both had followers (boyfriends) you see," said Violet, "though it were a big risk. We'd 'ave got the sack if we'd been caught. I used to see my young man—a corporal he was—in the saddle room in the stable yard. Now Ivy, she took hers up in the hay loft. He was a black 'un. I never did quite fancy a black 'un meself, but Ivy thought he was lovely."

When we parted, Violet gave me a souvenir mug of Queen Elizabeth's Golden Jubilee. I felt tears prick my eyes. It was a completed circle, replacing the Coronation mug Nanny had given me when we left Edwinstowe, and which had been lost or broken when my family moved south after the war.

In return, I gave Violet a cozy flannel-lined faux fur rug I'd made for her to keep her snug when she was watching television on cold winter nights.

She died in her sleep a few months later.

The day after our tea party with Violet I was welcomed back to Edwinstowe House with a charming little ceremony and presented with a book about my father. After lunch in the Canteen, (the old scullery), we were given the grand tour.

Everything was so changed that I only recognized our old nursery because of the bars still on the big window. The room was full of office equipment and young people clicking away at their computers. They all stopped work and turned to stare when they were told that I had grown up in the house. They made me feel as old-fashioned as a feather fan.

"You mean this was your *home?*" asked a girl with spiky orange hair. "Your family—like—*lived* here?"

"Doesn't it make you like—totally sad—to see what's happened to it?" someone else asked.

I thought about it. "Not really," I said, and realized as I spoke that it was true. For better or worse, the world I remembered had gone for ever, and I was glad that the grand old house had survived into the twenty-first century and, best of all, been instrumental in bringing renewed prosperity to the village.

"I bet there'll soon be a Starbucks in the village street," said my husband as we stepped into the elevator. It had replaced the graceful curving staircase down which my mother had once drifted on a cloud of *Quelques Fleurs* in her scarlet evening dress and silver sandals to flirt with Sir William.

Chapter 6

War Baby

I was seven when I met my brother Thomas for the first time, and he was about an hour old. The date was August 28, 1939, and The Second World War would break out six days later.

I'd known all morning that something unusual was afoot. Instead of getting on with their housework or hastening to answer one of the little bells on springs displayed in rows in a glass-fronted box outside the pantry, Ivy and Violet were hovering on the landing, talking in whispers.

Dr. Grey and Nanny and another woman I'd never seen before kept going in and out of my mother's room. My father hadn't left for his office, which was unusual on a week day. He was stamping about downstairs, looking fierce and shouting at the dogs.

I went to look for Johnny to see if he knew what was going on but I couldn't find him. He wasn't in the nursery, but a faint mewing told me he'd shut my kitten in the dolls' house again. I'd just got it out and comforted it and was trying to coax it to drink some milk from its saucer when Nanny came in and said, "You can run along to Mummy's room now and see your new brother. Remember to be very quiet."

A new brother? It was the first time I'd heard anything about any new brother. Where had they got him? How old was he? My first thought was that two brothers would mean more teasing and arm-twisting and even less chance of being allowed to bat at cricket. Why couldn't they have got a sister?

I opened my parents' bedroom door and slipped in. The first thing I saw was that their big carved walnut bed had been raised on bricks and completely draped in white sheets. The only sound in the room was a blue-bottle battering itself against the closed window. Instead of my mother's scent, there was an unpleasant sickly smell—chloroform, though I didn't know it then.

My mother was lying very still on the bed. Her eyes were closed and her fair hair was dark and wet-looking. Someone had combed it back off her forehead. You could see the comb's teeth marks.

She was Snow White in her glass coffin.

My father was standing at the foot of the bed, looking down at her. He seemed different somehow. Usually the centre of the known universe, at that moment he looked more like me—on the outside looking in.

Completely forgetting about the new brother I'd come to see, I went to stand beside him and slipped my hand into his.

"Is Mummy dead?" I asked him.

His hand twitched. He frowned down at me. "Dead? No, of course not. She's very tired. She's having a little sleep."

My mother was lying very still on the bed

"Like Snow White? After she pricked her finger?"

"What?"

"It was a spell. The wicked witch"—I paused and stared suspiciously at the unknown woman bending over the bed. She had a witch's mole on her cheek with hairs growing out of it. I tugged on my father's hand. "The witch cast a spell on her. Witches do that."

"What? What?" My father took his hand away and gestured to a blue basket I hadn't noticed before on a stand by the window. "Go and look at your new brother. His name is Thomas. Then run along and find Nanny."

I crossed the room and looked into the basket.

My new brother was a *baby*! Why hadn't Nanny said? I gazed at him, completely fascinated. I'd never seen a new baby close to before. He had no hair to speak of, but his eyelashes were longer than mine and lay on his cheeks like two silky fans. As I gazed at him, he yawned in his sleep and I saw that he had no teeth. I didn't know that new babies came without teeth. He'd better hurry up and get some or there'd be no Tooth Fairy for Thomas.

He unfurled one fist and stretched his fingers and I noticed that his tiny almost transparent nails needed cutting. I put a finger in his palm and his fingers closed round it like little tentacles. An unexpected lump rose in my throat and tears prickled in my nose. I was learning a big, confusing new lesson: *Love hurts.*

I leaned over the crib. My baby brother smelt like hot buttered toast. "Hello, Thomas," I whispered into his sweet little ear, "I'm your sister."

A heavy hand came down on my shoulder. It was the witch. She said, "Don't touch baby, dear. Off you go now."

"Are we going to keep him? For good? This baby?"

She laughed. "Well, of course!"

I took a closer look at her mole. "Is there a spell on Mummy?"

"A spell? You funny little thing! Run along and play now."

Thomas had arrived a month late. No wonder his nails needed cutting. I heard Violet telling Ivy that he weighed eleven pounds, the size of a three-month-old baby.

"Fancy that!" said Ivy, "poor Madam!" she added mysteriously.

His arrival that morning seemed to have disrupted the household even more than the coming war. Nanny wasn't in the nursery, so I went down to the kitchen to see if there was a cake bowl to lick out or any left-over pastry scraps for making into things.

For once the cook didn't chase me away. It was eleven o'clock and the gardeners were clattering into the scullery in their muddy boots for their mugs of sweet orange-coloured tea and doorsteps of bread and dripping. Puffed up with importance, the cook was announcing the arrival of "Master Thomas."

Then I heard her say: "Poor little mite, what a time to be born! They say them Jerries eat babies."

I froze. Last time I'd visited the kitchen I'd learned that 'them Jerries' (the Germans) were going to drop out of the sky on parachutes dressed as nuns with guns up their skirts and shoot the lot of us. But *eat babies*? Eat Thomas, with his bald little head and his tiny mottled fists?

Them Jerries would have me to reckon with first.

The most frightening place I knew of in the entire world was the goose

My baby brother, Thomas

house. If you ventured into their pen the geese would come running at you, their rubbery feet slapping the mud, their necks stretched out, hissing and ready to peck your legs if you weren't quick enough skipping out and slamming the rickety wooden door in their faces.

Luckily they had just been fed and were squabbling and guzzling away in their disgusting trough when I arrived on my mission. They ignored me as I slid the rusty bolt back and slipped through the door. My bare legs prickled with terror as I scurried across their pen and into the shed where they slept at night. Feeling my way in the gloom, I cleared the straw out of a nesting box at the back and replaced it with a cozy bed of my dolls' pram pillows and blankets.

If the Germans were half as scared of the geese as I was, my baby brother would be safe if I hid him there till—till when? Till we could escape? Till the war was over? This was too big a problem for me to wrestle with, so I didn't. Getting back out of the pen without being chased by the geese was enough of a challenge.

As I went back to the house I glanced up at the clear blue August sky. No nuns on parachutes yet.

It seemed that my mother was going to organize and direct the suddenly urgent preparations for the coming war from her bed. In those days you stayed in bed with your tummy tightly bound with wide linen bandages for a full month after the birth of a baby.

"No wonder you've got stretch marks," my mother said years later, inspecting my tummy as I lay sun-bathing in a bikini in the garden of their house in South Africa.

In a flurry of activity, black-out curtains were made for all the windows and one of the cellars was equipped with camp-beds and hurricane lamps. Pairs of red-painted buckets of sand and water were distributed along the corridors ready to put out fires started by incendiary bombs falling on the roof.

We were all issued with gas masks in little square boxes with shoulder straps and shown how to put them on and told to keep with us at all times, which of course we didn't after about two days.

My father gathered a rag-tag collection of villagers too old or infirm for military service and formed the village Home Guard. Men only, of course, in those days. He marched them up and down the drive with pitch forks and sticks and one or two shotguns on their shoulders and made them creep about, creaking and complaining, among the gorse bushes on the Common on maneuvers.

Major Monker from the Hall hung about on the fringes of these activities, hoping to be allowed to join in, but my father ignored him as usual. Poor Major Monker, he never understood that anyone below the rank of Colonel who used his military rank in civilian life, (especially if he'd been in the Army Pay Corps), was ever going to be acknowledged by my father, (blown up and gassed in the trenches in an infantry regiment). My father despised him and always referred to him as "that damned Monker feller."

The whole village was caught up in preparations for war. Shop windows were plastered with lattices of tape to prevent flying glass when the bombs began to fall and whooping test wails from the air raid siren frightened us out of our wits several times a day. Posters appeared everywhere warning, *Idle Talk Costs Lives!* I wondered if my mother's conversations on the telephone with her friends counted. I certainly hoped not. They often went on for hours. Another worrying poster demanded, *Is Your Journey Really Necessary?* and I thought about her weekly trips to Worksop to have her hair done.

Once Mr. Chamberlin had announced that England was at war, Johnny and I were required to sit quietly and listen to the 6 o'clock news every evening in the drawing room. The grown-ups' faces were solemn. Sometimes my mother had tears in her eyes. The news-reader had to say his name so we knew it wasn't wicked Lord Haw-Haw hoodwinking us with German lies and propaganda. "Here is the news and this is Alvar Lydell reading it." I heard the word *Soviet* mentioned quite often, which was puzzling. Surely the BBC ought to know better? Serviette was common. You were supposed to say table napkin. So much for my understanding of the events rocking the world.

One evening my mother turned pale and went to sit on the arm of my father's chair. He took her hand and patted it. The news-reader was saying:

"During last night's raid on London a well-known society nightspot, the Cafe de Paris, received a direct hit. A high explosive bomb came through the glass roof causing heavy casualties and killing everyone on the dance floor."

Years later, I learned that my parents had been dancing there the night before.

My sister Iris was seventeen when war broke out. She gave our parents no peace till they let her leave boarding school and join the Women's Land Army. For once she won our father's approval when she said she wanted to do her bit to help win the war. So home she came, having tossed her hated school hat out of the train window, her hair suspiciously blonde, her pockets finally empty of white mice. They'd had a disconcerting habit of appearing from the neck of her shirt and sitting on her shoulder washing their whiskers or poking a twitchy pink nose out of her sleeve, making the maids shriek.

I hardly recognized her. Overnight, or so it seemed, she had emerged from the chrysalis of her unbecoming school uniform and blossomed into a beauty along the lines of one of the goddesses in my book of Greek myths. She must have inherited her astonishing looks from her father, The Bounder. She certainly didn't look anything like the rest of us.

The Land Army didn't last long.

Poor Iris—an early victim of clever advertising—had fallen for the recruiting posters. They showed a winsome girl bottle-feeding a baby lamb in a cosy farmhouse kitchen or holding a sheaf of wheat in a sun-lit field or, fetchingly got up in jodhpurs and tight green sweater, exercising some gentleman farmer's hunter.

In reality she found herself stumbling out into the bitter pre-dawn darkness to slop buckets of pig-swill into troughs or dig up frozen turnips in a field—all the while fending off the amorous advances of a farmer who was no gentleman. She soon packed her bags and returned to Edwinstowe, where to her delight she found the whole place overrun with young men in pale blue uniforms.

To avoid the threat of evacuees from the East End of London, (the poor things, dreadful rumours preceded them about hair infested with nits and no clue as to the proper use of a knife and fork or a lavatory), my mother instead offered to allow the young men from the RAF airfield under construction nearby to use our swimming pool. Officers only, of course.

Iris was in seventh heaven. She was engaged and dis-engaged to be married every other week. It was just as well the young pilots weren't needed yet to chase the Luftwaffe from England's skies because most of them were camped out on our front doorstep.

The novelty of the air raid warnings soon wore off. They mostly turned out to be false alarms anyway, and my mother got sick of herding us all down to the cellars in the dead of night. I was rather sorry. Any disruption of nursery routine was always welcome.

One night while we were still expecting to be bombed at any minute, the siren must have interrupted a dinner party in full swing downstairs. I awoke to find myself in the arms of Iris's current fighter pilot fiancé, roped in to carry me from the night nursery down to the cellars. The draft blowing up the cellar steps was dank and clammy against my bed-warm feet. There was much giggling and scuffling in the semi-darkness, and all around the rustle and swish of long skirts, whiffs of different women's scent and the smell of cigars.

"I hope it's all right, I'm bringing my wine." said a female voice.

"Personally, I've brought the bottle," a man said. More laughter.

I kept my eyes closed in case I'd be put down and expected to walk.

Through my lashes I watched the swinging beam of a hurricane lamp darting from the silver buttons on the pale blue uniform against my cheek. I pretended my Prince had come to carry me off to his castle to live happily ever after. Nanny and her rules would be banned from the castle and no one would be allowed to eat animals.

From among her many suitors Iris eventually settled on black-mustached Ned, who roared up the drive to woo her in a noisy red sports car. Their engagement was announced, and preparations for the wedding went forward immediately. The war seemed to be bringing a slightly giddy sense of urgency to everything.

"I do hope dear Ned flies his Spitfire more carefully than he drives his motor car," remarked my mother one day as they shot off down the drive in a shower of gravel and clashing gears, narrowly missing Cartledge the groom, who was returning from exercising my father's hunter, Actress, who swerved nervously into the dahlias.

My sister Iris and Ned are married

Due to rationing and clothing coupons, the bride drifted up the aisle a few weeks later, a vision in a Scarlett O'Hara gown she'd designed herself and the village seamstress had run up out of a pair of cream brocade curtains Iris had unearthed from an attic.

No leave was being granted because of the war, so their honeymoon had to be postponed. Off went Iris to live in starry-eyed bliss among the concrete walkways and hastily knocked together prefabricated houses on the Base.

"Mummy, do you cook a rabbit with its fur coat on or off?" she rang up to ask one day.

"Just a minute, darling. I'll ask the cook," replied my mother, who naturally had no idea.

They never did have their honeymoon. Ned was killed over France five months later, and Iris lost the baby she was carrying. She was eighteen by then. Pale and sad, she came home with her boxes of un-used wedding presents and a withered carnation from her bouquet to her little attic bedroom known as the Crow's Nest.

But in no time at all she was quarreling with our father, and with the resilience of youth she soon cheered up and went off to enlist in the American Red Cross. War widows were allowed to choose what war-work they did for a year. Everyone else was conscripted.

"Why can't you join one of the *British* women's services?" demanded my father.

"I like the uniform best," said Iris, incurring a lecture on vanity and frivolity in times of war.

One of her American admirers gave Iris a black spaniel puppy whom she named Mossy and took everywhere with her. On a train crowded with military personnel traveling from Salisbury to London one day Mossy jumped from her lap onto the lap of a handsome Lieutenant in the Parachute Regiment seated opposite, and so Iris met Teve, who was to become her next husband.

The Servant Problem and rationing and food and clothing coupons were now the main topics of conversation between my mother and her friends. Servants were leaving domestic employment by the score, never to return. Dressed in trousers, their hair tied up in coloured scarves, *Music While You Work* blasting out over the racket of machinery, they much preferred the camaraderie and better wages to be found in the munitions factories, and who could blame them? I can't think why Ivy and Violet didn't leave too.

If Hitler's invasion plans for England included laying siege to Edwinstowe House, there'd have been enough food to keep us going for years. The newly constructed Store Cupboard's shelves were soon crammed with home-bottled fruit and vegetables, jams and jellies and chutneys, salted beans and tall earthenware jars of eggs preserved in something called Waterglass. From the rafters, a row of smoked hams from the

Home farm hung in muslin bags. My mother displayed the store cupboard to her friends in exactly the same way she used to show off a new hat.

"You are *wonderful*, Margot!" they cried admiringly, "Isn't she *marvellous*?" they asked each other as they trooped back to the drawing room for another gin and lime. Surely they don't think my mother had stained her own fingers with all that peeling and chopping and preserving?

But in spite of all the grumbling about ration books and the unavailability of oranges and soap flakes, people in the country—who mostly had access to locally grown fruit and vegetables and space to raise a few chickens and rabbits—never suffered the shortages and long queues of town-dwellers. Not to mention the horrors of being bombed night after night.

Sherwood Forest was transformed into one vast ammunition dump, and to the delight of the village girls a multi-national military camp sprang up on the edge of the village to guard it. The pub was jolted from its habitual slumber by swarms of free-spending "over-here, over-paid, and over-sexed" American, Canadian, and Australian soldiers and, seduced by glamorous uniforms and unlimited supplies of chocolate and cigarettes and silk stockings, the village girls abandoned their local boyfriends in droves and learned to jitter-bug. Brawling and fist fights and visits from the Military Police became commonplace, and a rash of illegitimate babies, some undeniably black, arrived in due course to shock the village busybodies.

"I thought them soldiers was here to defend us from the Jerries," grumbled the cook. "If you ask me they should've stopped at 'ome."

Rows of hump-backed galvanized metal Nissen storage huts soon stretched for miles beneath the oak trees, and tanks and trucks lumbered and crashed like prehistoric monsters through the bracken, leaving shattered trees and desolation in their wake.

Signs appeared everywhere warning: "Restricted Area. No Entry" and barbed wire fences were strung up and patrolled by armed guards with Alsatian dogs straining at their chain leashes.

But I thought about the Germans eating babies, and I was glad the soldiers had come. In spite of what they were doing to my beloved forest, and in spite of not being allowed to ride my pony there any more.

Chapter 7

Horse Heaven and Hunting Hell

When I was about four or five our groom Cartledge started teaching me to ride. Cartledge had been with my father during The Great War, and had stayed with him ever since. He was the archetypical groom right down to his bandy legs in their polished black leather gaiters, his checkered waistcoat, and his way of half-whistling half-hissing through his teeth when he was brushing a horse.

It was thanks to Cartledge that I learned to ride quite well and to respect and care for horses. Woe betide me if I forgot to check my pony's hooves for stones or brought her back to the stable yard sweating.

Part of my father's modernization programme at the mines included phasing out the use of pit ponies. Those poor ponies often lived and died underground, many of them eventually going blind, and all of them living in wretched and unnatural conditions. Luckily my Welsh pony, Beauty, had only been down the pit a short time when my father had her brought to the surface and gave her to me.

People seem to think Shetland ponies make ideal children's mounts because they are so small, quite overlooking their famously mean and stubborn natures. Beauty was twelve hands tall—considerably bigger than a Shetland—and she could be quite bossy and willful and capable of tipping me off if she thought I wasn't paying attention, but she had the sweetest and gentlest nature. Round as a hedgehog, she had elegantly slender legs and dainty hooves, a thick black mane, a tail that swept the ground when left un-trimmed, a charming retrousse nose, and dark liquid eyes framed with long black lashes. Her name suited her perfectly.

Keep your hands and your heels down,
Your head and your heart high,
Your knees into your horse's sides,
And your elbows into your own.

This jingle, taught to me by Cartledge, accompanied me round and round on the lunging rein during my riding lessons, Cartledge's long whip flicking at Beauty's fetlocks.

"Miss Diana, Miss Diana, what am I to do with you? I can read a newspaper between you and your 'oss!" he would bellow as the pennies I was supposed to be gripping between my knees and the saddle (and could keep if I succeeded) fell into the long grass.

Riding with Cartledge the groom

"You have to fall off thirty-nine times before you can call yourself an 'ossman," he'd say as he picked me up from yet another tumble when Beauty skidded to a halt, her neck stretched out over some small jump, and I went sailing over without her. Why thirty-nine times I never did discover.

After my lesson, Cartledge usually saddled my father's huge excitable hunter Actress and took her out to exercise her in Sherwood Forest. Before long I was allowed to accompany them, trotting along on the leading rein, Beauty's short legs trying valiantly to keep up with Actress's ranging gait.

By the time I was about six I had attained the level of "ossmanship" required by Cartledge to be trusted to go riding alone, (something that would surely be unthinkable today), and the green depths of the forest and all its myths and legends became my domain. Exploring its sandy trails and mossy paths, I could be Maid Marion, a gypsy princess, a spy, one of Enid Blyton's *Famous Five*.

In summer the bracken grew so high in places that I rode through spiky, bitter-scented green tunnels full of flickering sunshine and gnats and butterflies. Sometimes I had deer for company, slipping like phantoms between the oak trees. There were bluebell dells, mysterious pools of dark still water, colonies of rabbits, owls, and a curiously twisted tree known as 'Robin Hood's Larder'. Here, legend had it, mead-filled wine skins and haunches of venison once hung, ready for those merry Greenwood feasts.

The Major Oak

My favourite place of all was the nine-hundred-year-old Major Oak where Robin was reputed to have hidden from the Sheriff of Nottingham's men. Standing alone in a sandy clearing, its girth was so immense that when you squeezed through the narrow split in its trunk, (Robin must have been quite a small man), you entered a secret chamber, its floor soft and spongy with decomposing wood.

Leaving Beauty dozing on her feet, her bridle tied to a branch, I spent hours inside the ancient tree, the mush-roomy gloom lit by beams of light falling through holes and cracks in the bark. There I could escape Nanny's everlasting "don't care was made to care" and "are we in mourning? Just look at those black finger nails!" and forget the boredom of lessons with the current governess. Hidden from the world inside the Major Oak I was free to enter in my imagination into the epic adventures I'd read about, hearing the clash of staves, the whoosh of arrows, the stamp of hooves and jingle of harness, snatches of ghostly laughter, the notes of Robin Adair's lute.

Today there is a protective fence round the Major Oak and steel girders propping up its mighty branches. In summer a uniformed guard sits at a little table selling postcards to the tourists. They come by the coach-load to enjoy The Robin Hood Experience and buy plastic bows and arrows and bottles of Authentic Mead at the Visitors' Centre and have tea at Maid Marion's Tea Shoppe in the village. But for me as a child on my fat little pony, Sherwood forest became the equivalent of modern children's video games, television, iPods and cell phones: as essential as breathing.

So when the war started and the army commandeered the forest and I was banished from my paradise, not even my father could ignore my misery. Eventually he took pity on me and arranged special passes for me and for Mary Gray the doctor's daughter who sometimes came riding with me.

"Now," said my father, "these are the rules. You are to carry your passes at all times. Do not touch any military equipment. Do not talk to the soldiers. Do not dismount from your ponies. Is that understood?"

"Yes Daddy!" I would willingly have gone to live with the dreaded Mrs. Scafe in Mansfield Woodhouse and eaten mud pies for an entire week to earn that pass.

But one day Mary and I were cantering along a sandy trail when I spotted an interesting cylinder sticking out of the soft ground and quite forgot my father's rules. The object reminded me of the polished shell cases in his study and I decided to take it home for him. I was so grateful to him for my pass, and he wasn't an easy person to find presents for.

"Well you'll have to get off and get it," said Mary. "If I get off Silver she won't let me get back on again." She never missed an opportunity to remind me that Silver was half-Arab and highly strung, whereas Beauty was just a Welsh mountain pony.

Mary was supposed to be my friend—the only one I was allowed to have—but I didn't really like her very much. When she came to tea in the nursery she always took the biggest piece of cake, and once when we were attempting to smoke stolen cigarettes on our ponies in the forest and I dropped mine in Beauty's mane and set it on fire, Mary went and told her mother. Who of course told my mother.

I dismounted and tugged the metal object out of the ground and climbed back into the saddle with it. Up the drive I trotted with my trophy—and straight into a drama that even Johnny was quite proud to relate to his prep school friends.

My father was on the telephone when I knocked on his study door.

"Come in," he called.

"Look, Daddy," I said, "I've got a present for you!"

Still holding the phone to his ear, my father turned—and I knew at once there was something terribly wrong with my present.

I could hear a voice still quacking as he lay the receiver down on the desk and came towards me. I clutched his present to my chest and stepped back, nearly tripping over the rug.

"Do exactly as I say," said my father in the voice he used to calm nervous horses, "Stand quite still. Give—that—to me. Good. Now, leave the room. Don't slam the door. Go and tell everyone in the house to go outside immediately. Do you understand?"

"Yes, Daddy."

I never did discover the exact nature of my unwelcome gift, but I did overhear my father saying to my mother, "...according to the chap from the Bomb Disposal Squad the damn thing could have gone off at any moment." I decided in the circumstances it was better not to mention dropping it on the road on the way home.

My pass to ride in the forest was withdrawn, but only for a week.

I got through the time re-reading a favourite book in which a little girl went into a dark corner of her pony's stable and whispered, "silver snaffles," and passed through the wall into a magical world where horses could talk and there were no grown-ups to worry about. I didn't wonder how she got back again, and the book didn't say.

"Silver snaffles. Silver snaffles." It was no use. However often I tried it, all I got were splinters in my groping fingers from the rough wooden planks in the darkest corner of Beauty's loose box.

Johnny had been taught to ride on Beauty too, but like many boys he showed little interest in riding or horses. Nevertheless, one day Jugo arrived in the stables and it seemed that Johnny was expected to ride him. What was our father thinking of? The only thing Jugo had in common with Beauty was that they were both ex-pit ponies. Poor Jugo, he couldn't help being an ugly dock-tailed cob with a bristly mane like a worn-out toothbrush, and I suppose his treatment underground probably accounted for his evil temper, but the fact remained I was terrified of his gnashing teeth and lashing hooves. If we did manage to get a saddle on him and dared to try to ride him he had a nasty habit of lying down and rolling on us without the slightest warning or provocation. Even Johnny was scared of him.

Our father had zero tolerance of any hint of cowardice on the part of his children. "Rubbish," he'd say when told of Jugo's latest vicious behaviour, "he just needs a firm hand."

One Saturday morning our father arrived in the stable yard to see what all the fuss was about. Taking the saddle from Johnny, he and strode over to Jugo. "Stand, boy," he ordered. Jugo flattened his ears and showed the whites of his eyes and my father slapped the saddle on his back. Jugo froze.

Then, as my father bent to reach for the girth under his belly, he went mad, rearing back and yanking the iron ring his halter was tied to out of the wall, landing a kick on my father's knee, (breaking his knee-cap it was later discovered), and cantering off out of the yard with a great clatter of hooves, his stubby tail in the air.

The next morning, Jugo was gone, and though I worried about his fate, I couldn't truthfully say I was sorry.

Early one bright winter morning I had a shock when I came out to the stables, intending to go for a ride in the forest. Beauty was standing out in the yard, already saddled. Her glossy dark bear-like winter coat had been clipped, leaving her oddly naked and diminished and mole-coloured. Her tail had been trimmed up to her hocks and her mane stood along her neck in a row of chunky little plaits. I hardly recognized her.

"Your father says you can start hunting," Cartledge explained. "Just two hours your first time out, mind," he added.

I saw that Actress had been similarly clipped and her mane plaited to conform to Cartledge's strict hunting standards. Cartledge himself was smartly turned out, complete with a bowler hat I'd never seen before. He inspected and grudgingly approved my usual jodhpurs and boots and hacking jacket, though I knew he considered them to be unladylike. He'd very much wanted to teach me to ride side-saddle.

The Meet was at Edwinstowe Hall, the home of the despised Major Monker. When we arrived and Beauty saw the other horses and riders milling about on the gravel drive and the swirl of barking hounds and sensed the general air of anticipation, she began dancing sideways and snatching at her bit and it was all I could do to control her.

"Steady there," said watchful Cartledge, though I could see he was having almost as much trouble with Actress.

A couple of maids from the Hall were moving rather nervously among the horses and riders, collecting the small silver mugs that had been used to serve the traditional Stirrup Cup.

Led by the Master of Foxhounds on a magnificent chestnut gelding, the hunt servants in their pink (actually scarlet) coats moved the hounds out and the rest of us followed. The hounds found a fox in the first copse of trees they drew, and in no time we were all galloping hell-for-leather across a ploughed field, clods of mud flying everywhere.

"Follow me!" Cartledge shouted as Actress jumped a low hedge, and over went Beauty and I and off again up a steep pasture. Then I saw we were approaching a really high hedge—far higher than anything Beauty and I had ever jumped before—but she was so excited I couldn't make her obey when Cartledge shouted a warning and turned Actress aside.

I felt my brave little pony gather herself under me and she leapt valiantly up at the towering hedge, following close behind the broad haunches of a huge grey mare—who luckily knocked a small gap in it. Somehow we cleared the hedge, but the unexpected ditch on the other side was too much for Beauty and she stumbled and fell and I landed on my back in the bottom of the ditch.

I saw her scramble to her feet and gallop on, reins and stirrups flapping, then everything else vanished as the rest of the field came thundering and grunting over where I lay—horses' under-bellies and girths darkened and foamed with sweat, boots and spurs in stirrups, hooves flashing a few inches from my head, lumps of earth and bits of hedge pelting down on me.

Then they were gone and I could hear a woodpecker hammering in the sudden silence.

Cartledge must have jumped the hedge somewhere else and caught up with Beauty. He was leading her when I wiped some of the mud out of my eyes with my sleeve and saw him looming above me on Actress. He dismounted and climbed down and helped me out of the ditch. He wiped my face with his handkerchief and picked some twigs out of my hair, and once he'd assured himself I wasn't hurt a broad, approving grin spread over his face. "Well," he said, "I'm right proud of the two of you! I'd never have thought that little 'un would have jumped like that, and you did well to stay with her." I glowed with pride

As I climbed back into the saddle Beauty's head went up at the call of the now distant horn, but it seemed that was to be the end of our first day's hunting. But I trotted home quite happily beside Cartledge, still basking in his rare praise.

"Well," said Nanny, "Straight into the bath with you!"

The next Saturday when we went out Beauty and I didn't come to grief over any jumps, in fact we kept up well with the rest of the field—and thus I learned that hunting wasn't only about the baying of the hounds and the creak of leather and the clean smell of horse-sweat. Nor was it just about the infectious excitement of galloping across the countryside with other horses and riders all jostling for position, or the thrill of flying over hedges and fences you didn't know you could possibly jump.

Somehow I had failed to realize the fox's role in the hunt, or have any notion of its barbaric death—pulled down and torn to pieces by twenty-two blood-crazed hounds. Even if it reached its lair, I learned later, it wasn't safe. A terrier carried on the pommel of one of the hunt servants' saddles would be put down the burrow to flush it out to face its tormentors.

On that day I witnessed the hunt servants jump off their horses and drive the hounds back so they could cut off the fox's head and paws and tail to be awarded as trophies. The bloody remains were tossed back into the frenzied pack.

Shocked and sickened, I watched the Master of Foxhounds ride over to a woman mounted sidesaddle on a great black horse who was standing with his head down, his sides heaving after the chase, his neck and chest lathered white with sweat. Her dark green riding habit and the white stock at her throat and the veil holding on her top hat were all splashed with mud and she was laughing and joking with her companions, apparently quite unmoved by the fate of the fox.

The Master reined in his horse beside her and leaned out of his saddle and daubed one of the fox's paws on the woman's face, smearing it with blood—*and she smiled!*

"First time in at the kill," Cartledge whispered beside me. "It's called being blooded."

Through waves of nausea I saw that the Master was now riding over to me. He had a big red face and he was smiling directly down at me. Blood had dripped from the severed paw in his hand onto his mud-splattered white britches.

Feeling the vomit rise in my throat, I yanked Beauty's head round and for the only time in my life I hit her hard on her rump with my riding crop. Startled, she jumped forward and although I knew how tired she was, she broke into a fast canter and we fled the scene.

That was the second and last time I ever went fox hunting, and to this day I'm ashamed that I ever went all.

Chapter 8

Village Life

If you didn't happen to love it, I suppose Edwinstowe was just another undistinguished little Nottinghamshire mining village, although the district's name—The Dukeries—did hint at illustrious connections.

There were several ducal mansions in the area, though I only ever remember going to Welbeck Abbey, the stately and intimidating home of the stately and intimidating Duke of Portland, where we were occasionally bidden to children's parties.

I dreaded those parties nearly as much as visits to the dentist. (Where you hoped your appointment would be in the morning, before appropriately named Mr. Hole got tired and began to peddle his drill more slowly.) I was beyond shy. I wished I could live in a wood with Mrs. Tiggy-Winkle and Little Grey Rabbit or in a jungle like Tarzan with a chimpanzee for a friend.

I never knew what to say if some child or footman spoke to me at those Welbeck Abbey parties, and not having any friends of my age or any social skills I didn't know the rules of any of the games we were required to play after tea. Musical Chairs, Sardines, Hunt the Slipper or Pass the Parcel. I was always last to be picked for any team, the first out, and often found myself wandering along deserted stone-flagged corridors lined with suits of armour and ancestral portraits, wondering where everyone had gone.

I did have a few friends in the village however, one of whom was Mrs. Grundy. She kept a dark, cave-like little shop where she sold newspapers and tobacco and sweets and a few toys and an odd assortment of such things as bicycle clips and fountain pens and wooden clothes pegs.

Mrs. Grundy was famous for her "bad legs" and for the rude language and unpredictable temper of the grey parrot who lived in a cage on the counter and scattered feathers and peanut shells over everything.

"How are your legs today, Mrs. Grundy?"

"How are your legs today, Mrs. Grundy?"

"Wouldn't wish 'em on me worst enemy, my duck," Mrs. Grundy would wheeze round her soggy Woodbine cigarette as she shuffled to the counter in her bedroom slippers. "Keep your fingers out of that cage if you don't want a good peck. What can I get for you today?"

For a half-penny you could buy a paper cornet of sugary multi-coloured Dolly Mixture scooped out of a tall glass jar with a tin shovel, or a stick of barley sugar, or a Gob Stopper nearly as big as a ping-pong ball which changed colour as you sucked it. If you had tuppence you could buy a brightly coloured paper bird on a string and stick which whistled when you whirled it round your head. They soon broke, and were buried under the blackberry bushes.

The decision of what to buy was always difficult, but Mrs. Grundy's patience was saintly.

"Bugger off!" her parrot would shout after me as I finally left the shop with my purchase, the little bell on the door going "ping" behind me.

I liked jolly Mr. Bostock the grocer very much too. He had red hair like a brush, and wore a spotless long white apron and stretchy metal bands round his shirt sleeves and liked to "get a breath of air" on his doorstep when he wasn't serving a customer. His shop smelt of spices and of the fresh sawdust on the floor. I was always happy to be sent round by the cook with the ration books and a list of things she'd forgotten to order. I loved watching Mr. Bostock cut a piece of cheddar cheese with a wire, weigh eight ounces of sugar into a blue bag, slice six rashers of bacon with the great silver wheel and lay them with a flourish on a piece of greaseproof paper.

I wonder what he'd have thought of the pre-packaged goods on today's supermarket shelves; the forty different cereals to choose from, the rows of cans and packets, the freezers stuffed with brightly wrapped pre-cooked meals and twenty-four flavours of ice cream, the sliced bread and cartons of orange and grapefruit juice, ten different products for cleaning the bathroom, the out-of-season grapes and strawberries and things he'd probably never even heard of such as cheeses from Switzerland or avocados.

Mr. Bostock the grocer

With a conspiratorial wink, Mr. Bostock would sometimes reach under the counter for an extra packet of rationed tea or a bar of soap he was saving for favoured customers like my mother, and slip it into my basket with my purchases. And almost always he'd take down a tin of broken biscuits, (sold at half-price), and give me a handful or, if I was really lucky, a small bag of Smith's Potato Crisps with its own little blue paper twist of salt inside.

I also loved taking Beauty to be shod by my hero of iron and fire, the village blacksmith. A muscular giant in a leather apron, he threw off spectacular great arcs of sweat as he pumped the bellows and thrust a new shoe into the flames with a pair of long pincers till it glowed red and then white. Sparks and sweat flew in all directions as he hammered and shaped the glowing shoe on the anvil, and steam hissed and billowed up into the blackened rafters when he plunged it into a vat of dark water.

The acrid smell of burning stung my nose as he tested the shoe against Beauty's neatly trimmed hoof. "Keep still there!" he'd shout through a mouthful of square-headed nails as he hammered a new shoe on, twisting the nail ends off with the other end of the hammer and rasping everything smooth with a big file.

Children loitered in the doorway, hens wandered in to peck and cluck among the hoof parings on the cobblestone floor, and the blacksmith whistled and sang and shouted friendly abuse at horses and hens and children alike as he worked. I sat quietly on an upturned bucket in a corner, enthralled by the whole performance. What child wouldn't be?

The job finished, the blacksmith wiped Beauty's hooves over with the same oily rag he used to mop his brow and led her out into the yard and swung me up onto her bare back as if I weighed no more than a rag doll. With a final slap on her rump he'd stride back into his forge and begin shouting, "Get over, there!" at some huge cart horse patiently waiting its turn.

Trotting home along the village street, I always hoped to reach the safety of the stable yard without encountering Our-Edly and his gang. If any of the miners' wives were attending to their babies in their prams on front doorsteps, or leaning on their garden gates among the nodding hollyhocks gossiping with their neighbours, I knew I was fairly safe. The most Our-Edly would risk then would be a bit of mild verbal abuse along the lines of: "Look who's 'ere! If it ain't Lady Muck 'erself!"

My hero of iron and fire, the village blacksmith

But my favourite village person of all was Nanny in her other life—the life she lived with her coal miner husband and grown-up son and daughter in one of the red brick semi-detached houses in the New Village.

I never did understand how she managed those two separate lives, for it seemed to me she was always in the nursery, her comforting presence there both night and day if one of us was ill. She always came on annual summer holidays to the sea with us, and was always there for Christmas and birthdays and Hot Cross Buns at Easter. When was she at home with her family?

Occasionally, as a special treat or reward for good behaviour, Nanny invited Johnny and me to tea at her house.

Without her cap, dressed in a skirt and jumper instead of her familiar starched white uniform, she became a completely different person. She was our hostess and we were her guests. She never said: "Sit up straight," or "Don't talk with your mouth full."

Once back in the nursery however, nothing was changed: "Drink up your milk. There's many would be glad of it." "Elbows!" It was a bit like my father's description of Christmas Day during The Great War. He said the German and British soldiers laid down their weapons and climbed out of their trenches and met in the mud and shell craters of Non-Man's-Land and shared food and cigarettes and showed each other photos of their sweethearts and families.

Then they got back in their trenches and went on blowing each other to smithereens.

The kettle was always steaming on the back of the hob at Nanny's house and everything was polished and starched and gleaming. There were delicious smells of homemade flapjack, currant buns, fresh lemon curd, and jars of strawberry or plum jam often cooling on the window-sill. When did she find time to do all that?

Today's women, juggling careers and marriages and children, seem to think they invented the stresses of the double life. Nanny was doing it with evident success—and without the aid of washing machines and deep freezes and convenience foods and a car to get about in—back in the 1940s.

Two scuffed brown leatherette chairs stood on either side of the shining black-leaded range in Nanny's kitchen, and before the hearth lay a multi-coloured rag rug which I much preferred to the faded Persian ones at home. The rest of the furniture was similar to that in the maids' sitting room at home; a varnished dresser and chairs, a table covered with a fringed red velvet cloth, a row of souvenir mugs of the Coronation or inscribed "A Present from Skegness" on the mantle.

The only other room downstairs, the Front Room, was never used and we were only allowed to peep inside. It smelt of lemon furniture polish and the soot which fell down the chimney onto the white paper fan in the tiny grate. There was a Three Piece Suite, its ginger upholstery protected (from what?) by white crocheted antimacassars on the arms and backs.

On the window-sill a china Alsatian dog and a ballerina daintily holding up her skirts turned their backs on the room and looked out onto the street from between looped-up net curtains. The unlined ginger brocade curtains were hung with the right side facing the street. The floral linoleum shone like a skating rink.

We were never invited to see upstairs.

In the days before my father's new pithead baths were built, when Nanny's husband Bear came shambling up the garden path at the end of his shift down the pit he was black from head to foot—except for the gleam of his teeth when he saw us waving to him from the window.

He wasn't allowed in the kitchen till he'd taken off his outer clothes in the scullery and washed and put on his carpet slippers. Poor Bear, he never came quite clean. His skin was pocked and ingrained with coal dust that no amount of scrubbing could remove. The same dust was also settling in his lungs, and would eventually kill him.

We called him Bear because he was bear-sized, and because, tired though he must often have been, he never minded getting down on the floor on all fours and letting us ride in and out of the furniture on his broad back. His huge, black-creased fingers were as delicate as a surgeon's when it came to mending dolls' house furniture or putting a lead soldier's head back on with a matchstick.

We called him "Bear"

My father didn't approve of education for girls.

"What's the use of teaching them Latin and Greek?" he demanded. "They only go off and get married."

He apparently saw no inconsistency in his views on raising daughters when my seventeenth birthday was approaching and he was heard to snort, "A Coming Out Ball? The Season? What the devil for? So she can go off and marry some chinless wonder? No child of mine is going near *that* meat market!"

I can't help wondering if his Scottish blood didn't rebel rather, hearing his friends grumble about the frightful cost of launching a daughter into London Society. In the event I neither received an education nor made my curtsy to the King at Queen Charlotte's Ball. But then, I didn't marry a chinless wonder either.

As there seemed to be no question of our going to the village school, we were taught by a series of more or less identical governesses. After Johnny went away to prep school when he was eight, I had lessons by myself.

Beige-coloured, humble, self-effacing creatures, those poor governesses must have had a perfectly wretched time. The maids thought they were stuck-up and resented the extra work, banging their meals down rudely on tin trays in their rooms, and Nanny ignored them completely, being much more interested in our bowels than our brains.

There we'd slump at the battered nursery table, yawning and fidgeting, chewing our pencils, feet wound round our chair legs, easily distracted by spilt paint water, the whinny of a pony or the arrival of a bumble bee through the open window in summer, bored to death, learning nothing if we could help it.

Of all the cavalcade of governesses to arrive with such timid aspirations and depart with such a crushed air of defeat, I can only recall two; one, only because she smelt so overpoweringly of dog biscuits. Did she eat them? Grind them down and powder her long sad dog-biscuit-coloured face with them? Keep them in her pocket to bribe my father's disdainful gun dogs? I never found out, and she didn't last long.

Then there was Miss Lindley. Unlike her predecessors, she was young and pretty and pranced around in bright clothes and lots of flying scarves. She charmed the maids, who put lace cloths on her tin trays and lent her

Dogbiscuits, Johnny and me

their copies of *Home Chat*, and somehow managed to get on the right side of Nanny. Even our father, previously never seen in the nursery, took to dropping in occasionally to see how our lessons were going.

We were Miss Lindley's instant slaves when it became clear that time-tables and conventional lessons bored her as much as they did us. "Come along children, get your Wellingtons on!" she'd cry clapping her hands, and off we'd go for a biology lesson in the stream. *Lambs Tales from Shakespeare* was cast cheerfully into the back of a cupboard. "Let's wait till you're old enough for the real thing," said Miss Lindley, and introduced us instead to *Huckleberry Finn* and Long John Silver and "Do you Remember an Inn, Miranda? Do you Remember an Inn?" "…and the fleas that tease in the High Pyrenees"…how I loved that poem.

In fact the only thing we were ever to hold against Miss Lindley was the Nursery Play.

My father came into the nursery during a spirited rehearsal one day and sat there laughing till the tears ran down his face. "I expect you'll be opening at the Theatre Royal in Nottingham soon," he said, taking out his hankie and mopping his eyes.

I showed him the invitations I was making. "We're going to ask you and Mummy and Nanny and the maids and Herbert and Cartledge and the gardeners," I explained.

"What a waste that would be," said my father. And the next thing we knew, footlights were being hired, Herbert was banging away in the dining room building a stage and some quite ambitious scenery, and the local dressmaker was sewing us costumes from our mother's discarded frocks; a long blue silk dress with white fur round the neck and hem for me, and a very dashing crimson and purple doublet and hose outfit for Johnny.

To our alarm our parents then invited about fifty of their friends to a cocktail party, with our theatrical offering as a sort of embarrassing hors d'oeuvres.

The whole thing was apparently a huge success—especially when the Queen of the Fairies knickers fell down during a piping rendition of *Cherry Ripe*, (actually *Chewwy Wipe*; I was still having trouble with my r's), and when Johnny sprang through a plywood window brandishing a cardboard sword and brought down the entire canvas backdrop to reveal Herbert in his braces taking a quick swig of whiskey out of one of the decanters on the dining room sideboard.

Although my formal education was limited, (to this day I have trouble adding up a column of figures, and don't even ask me about fractions or long division or the main rivers of South America), I picked up a certain amount of useful—and a lot of puzzling and incomprehensible—information on my illicit afternoon visits to the maids' sitting room.

Unlike the rest of the house, which rang with my father's cries of "Fug rats!" as he strode about throwing windows open even during raging blizzards, the windows in the maids' sitting room, where my father never penetrated, were kept hermetically sealed and a bright coal fire blazed winter and summer in the small black-leaded grate

Enthroned in the best chair by the fire, the cook of the moment presided over a brown teapot in a purple and orange crocheted crinoline-lady tea cozy which I greatly admired. In a dresser under the window were bits of complicated lacy mauve and acid green knitting, starched uniform collars and cuffs, rude post cards from Blackpool depicting fat ladies at the seaside, packets of stale biscuits, hairnets, and tattered copies of *Home Chat*, from whose pages I gleaned my first misleading notions of romantic love. *She trembled as he swept her into his masterful embrace....*

The only thing I didn't like in the whole room was a picture on the wall of two jolly monks tucking into what I took to be a big plate of worms. I'd never seen spaghetti, which would no doubt have been condemned by my father as "foreign muck."

Thursday afternoons were best of all in the maids' sitting room. I'd slip unnoticed under the balding green velvet cloth on the table in the corner and settle down among the balls of fluff on the linoleum for a fascinating session of eavesdropping.

On Thursdays the village hairdresser, (nicknamed Twizzly-Lizzy by my father) arrived with all the latest gossip, the tools of her trade packed in a cardboard suitcase. With a pair of metal tongs heated to a dull glow in a mentholated spirit flame, Twizzly-Lizzy would transform Ivy and Violet's limp brown hair into fashionable rows of little sausages ready for whatever giddy adventures awaited them on their respective half-days out.

No wonder my mother went to Worksop to get her hair done; the smell of singeing hair on Thursday afternoons quite overpowered the normal maids' sitting room smells of Californian Poppy scent and stewed tea and peppermints and armpits.

"They say that little madam Dawn Stiggins is in the family way." Twizzy-Lizzy would begin as she laid out her equipment.

"She's never!" The cook's mouth drew up like a dog's behind.

"They say it's one of them black American soldiers up at t' camp." said Twizzy-Lizzy amid small puffs of steam and smoke beginning to rise from Ivy's head.

"Well! I go to our 'ouse!" said Violet (a local expression denoting astonishment).

"P'raps she'll go and live in 'ollywood!" ventured the spotty little scullery maid enviously.

"Don't talk so daft," snapped the cook. "No better than she ought to be, that one. Didn't I always say she'd come to a bad end? Flaunting 'erself in them American silk stockings."

"It's the mother I feel sorry for, the poor soul." said Ivy, pulling out a temporary curl and admiring it in the hand mirror as it sprang back.

I loved those conversations. It didn't matter in the least that often I hadn't the slightest idea what they were about.

Later, at tea in the nursery: "Nanny, what's 'in the family way'?"

"Ask no questions you'll hear no lies. Eat up those crusts. They'll make your hair curl."

'Twizzly-Lizzy' arrived with all the latest gossip . . .

Chapter 9

Seldom Seen or Heard

Unfortunately for me I was born too early to reap the benefits of today's indulged and entitled children. Our father's gun dogs got more attention and better parts in our home movies than his children did.

In contrast, modern children—encouraged and applauded by their parents—occupy center stage and hog the limelight (both in real life and on videos and in photo albums) from the first chocolate-birthday-cake-in-the-hair to the wedding cake—and beyond.

Some flickering black-and-white home movies shot at Edwinstowe which came to light recently in an old trunk and were transferred to DVD show the very different pecking order which prevailed at Edwinstowe. They are concerned almost exclusively with one person—my father. We see him, natty in plus-four trousers and long Argyle socks, whacking golf balls. Here he is, holding a salmon he's just hauled out of some Scottish river up to the camera. There, diving into the pool at the Hotel du Cap in the South of France in a terrible striped bathing suit. Next he's peppering skies full of pheasants, Herbert reloading the Purdeys at his shoulder. Now he's squinting in the sun as he pulls up a sail. Here he comes again, followed by my mother, both got up in full tropical regalia including pith helmets, traipsing down the gangplank of some cruise ship in Sierra Leone.

Johnny and I were mere bit players in those films and, I suppose, in our parents' lives too. Occasionally we are to be glimpsed running across a sunlit lawn, splashing in the shallow end of the swimming pool, or trotting off down the drive on our ponies—usually to finish up a roll of film. Thomas's babyhood wasn't recorded at all. Perhaps the camera broke, or you couldn't get film during the war.

There is one short episode in which my father is seen sitting on a garden bench, fooling with his dogs. When I come toddling up in my little velvet collared coat, blond curls bobbing, age about three, you can almost hear my mother behind the camera calling: "Well pick her up, darling! Sit her on your knee or something!" After some hesitation my father does so, and we both stare rather anxiously at the camera. That must be one of the few times I ever sat on my father's knee.

Though we children were largely ignored and left in the care of other people who were paid to look after us, I suppose Sir William was right when he reminded us, (the time we nearly hung Our-Edly in the ponies' shed), that we lived in—or at any rate on the fringes of—a world of privilege. The Great Depression, poverty, unemployment, and even the worst atrocities of The Second World War seem, in retrospect, to have been little more than passing clouds in the sunny skies of my parents' carefree lives. I don't suppose this is entirely true, merely my childish perspective. But still, to a great extent they were definitely insulated by class, geography, my father's important work, reasonable wealth—and a certain attitude of superiority encouraged by membership of that exclusive club: The Empire upon which the sun never, at that time, seemed likely to set.

"Oh well, at least I can't blame my parents if I'm a mess," I said to a friend who was banging on recently about her wretched childhood, "I hardly ever saw them."

"That's another form of child abuse," she retorted.

I didn't argue because she'd read all the books and I hadn't, but I didn't agree with her. I think we were lucky to have had Nanny. At least you always knew where you were with her. Counting on our mother to look after us would have been utterly nerve-wracking. She would have been about as reliable as a pretty butterfly with painted wings hovering in the sunshine; here today, gone tomorrow. And as for my father—the briefest exposure to his alarming presence sucked all the oxygen out of the air leaving you gasping like a mackerel in the bottom of a fishing boat.

A typical example of my father's effect on me was his one attempt to teach me to swim. He so traumatized me that I never went in our swimming pool again if I could help it, and didn't learn to swim till I was forty. His method of teaching was to dangle me in the icy cold pool on the end of a sort of fishing pole contraption with an old dog collar round my waist and walk along the edge of the pool towing me through the water shouting, "Kick with your legs! Keep your fingers together!"

From time to time he slackened the line to check my progress and down I went into the depths like a sack of potatoes. Eventually he gave up and dragged me out of the pool, spluttering and shivering and choking and half drowned, and handed me back to Nanny in disgrace.

One blissful year the swimming pool was out of commission for the entire summer, removing the danger of any more swimming lessons. In a bizarre attempt to turn the pool into a sort of Midlands Mediterranean, my father caused a whole truckload of salt to be dumped into the water which—as anyone could have told him if he'd have listened—corroded all the pipes and the pump and the filtering system, and half the garden had to be dug up in consequence.

Whenever my parents went away, which they did quite often until the war put a stop to their travels abroad, my mother would always clasp us to her and burst into heart-rending tears before allowing herself to be handed into the car and tucked up in fur rugs by Herbert. Then we'd stand on the drive with Nanny and wave, and off they'd go to Victoria Station to catch the Golden Arrow to Paris and the South of France, or to Southampton to board some cruise ship.

Seeing so little of my mother anyway, I didn't miss her in the least once the dramatics of her departure were over. I'm sorry to say that if I thought about her at all when she was gone it was only to wonder what she might bring back for us. Once it was a brown velvet, grass-skirted, Zulu doll taller than me that she'd won in a ship's raffle, another time a branch with real oranges growing on it.

If it had been Nanny my father was whisking off, that would have been—as she herself might have said—a very different kettle of fish.

This may sound exaggerated, but it's a perfectly true story: Years later when my parents were over on a visit to England from their home in South Africa, I became slightly annoyed by my mother's criticism of the admittedly amateur way in which I was bringing up my three young children.

"How come you're such an expert?" I eventually burst out, "You hardly ever even *saw* us when we were this age!"

"Darling!" she cried, quite offended, "How can you say such a thing? Why, I always had lunch in the nursery on Thursdays!"

We didn't really see much more of our parents on the annual Bucket and Spade summer holidays at the seaside, although those holidays were arranged—and continued even during war years—entirely for our benefit, it being considered that growing children "needed sea air." Well, to be sure sea air was probably better for us than Nanny's conviction that inhaling the fumes of the boiling tar used to repair the road was "good for our chests" and would prevent whooping cough. She always rushed us out into the street whenever she heard the grinding rumble of the steam roller approaching.

The summer exodus to the sea involved the entire household being packed up and driven in a convoy of cars (*Is Your Journey Really Necessary?*) and a removal van to the East Coast or the Isle of Wight or North Wales. The removal van was needed because my mother refused to stay in a rented house without her own bed. On one occasion when the great hulking thing couldn't be got up the stairs of a house in Totland Bay she refused to get out of the car.

"You'll just have to find us somewhere else," she said to my father, "otherwise I'm going home."

My father's loathsome boat also had to be moved to a new location each summer. That first magical glimpse of the sea was always spoilt for me by the sight of *Sea Scout* anchored off the beach, biding her time. She was an ugly top-heavy cabin-cruiser and we all hated her. My father had had her built to his own specifications in the Isle of Wight, so naturally he would-n't hear a word against her. She rolled alarmingly in the smallest sea, she was sluggish under sail, and her engine was always breaking down amid torrents of oaths never usually heard on our father's lips. My mother sensi-bly refused to set foot on *Sea Scout*, and eventually my father gave up try-ing to turn me into a crew member. Scorned and despised like my Labrador, Suzy, (given to me because she turned out to be gun-shy), I was condemned as "a bad sailor."

I've since crossed the Pacific Ocean from California to Hawaii in huge seas on a racing yacht without a hint of sea sickness. It was my father's "No, no *no! Not* that line, you little fool!" or, "How many times have I told you to *duck* when we go about?" or, "Come here. It's about time you learned to take your own fish off the hook" that sent me bolting to the side to be sick out of sheer fright.

One summer my father and I went down to Wales in advance of the rest of the family. I'd had an operation to straighten my snaggled front teeth, and it was thought that the famous benefits of sea air would hasten my recovery.

Was it any wonder I was wasting away? I wasn't allowed to take my new dental plate out even for

Johnny and I at the seaside

meals and it felt as if I'd got a mousetrap in my mouth. No one seemed to have noticed that I hadn't been able to eat anything that needed chewing since I came out of hospital.

We set off in my father's smart pearl grey Packard in polite and uneasy silence. The car's smooth American suspension meant that we had to stop several times for me to be sick before we'd even got as far as Chester. My poor father, he couldn't have had the faintest idea how to cope with a tongue-tied twelve-year-old child staring fixedly out of the window, smelling faintly of vomit. He must have been regretting the whole idea long before we arrived in Wales.

That year we were to occupy the whole of Mrs. Jones' boarding house in the small fishing village of Llanbedrog. I was given a stuffy cupboard of a room under the eaves with a magical view over the treetops to a sandy cove and the sea. It would have been a view to delight my heart—if only *Sea Scout* hadn't been rocking at anchor in the middle of it.

Mrs. Jones was a motherly soul in a flowered pinafore. She cooked us fresh mackerel for supper, complete with heads and tails and milky dead eyes. I tried my best to eat a bit of it but I was sick again before I went to bed.

My heart sank at breakfast when my father announced that we were taking a picnic and going out *for the whole day* on *Sea Scout*.

"That'll put roses in her cheeks, the poor little thing!" cried Mrs. Jones, handing us a hamper of food.

By some miracle the morning passed without me disgracing myself or my father losing his temper, and by the time we dropped anchor in a deserted bay to have lunch he was in high spirits.

"I should take that thing out of your mouth if I were you," he said, noticing me trying to nibble round the edges of a sandwich. I levered the hated contraption off my teeth and wrapped it carefully in my hankie and bolted down the first solid food I'd had in about three weeks.

The sun fell warmly through my Aertex shirt. Little wavelets slapped against *Sea Scout*'s fresh white paint. Gulls screamed and swooped for the bits of bread we threw to them. Happiness stole cautiously over me.

Then disaster struck.

Picking up a towel to shake the last picnic crumbs overboard, I saw my dental plate—still wrapped in my hankie—fall into the dark green water and sink slowly from view.

My father's wrath was something to behold. "You will sit there and fish for it till you catch it," he thundered, surely with little hope of success, "Do you realize that plate cost *forty pounds*?"

As if I'd wanted the beastly thing in the first place.

Needless to say that was the last we saw of my plate. It was getting dark by the time we returned in stormy silence to Mrs. Jones' boarding house. I was sent straight to bed in disgrace. Not that I minded. I was exhausted and sunburned and I had a bad pain in my tummy.

During the night I had to keep getting up and creeping downstairs to be sick in the rather horrid cracked and stained lavatory on the floor below. (When my mother eventually arrived in Wales and saw that lavatory she refused to stay at Mrs. Jones' boarding house. Anyhow her bed would never have gone up the stairs.) In the morning I couldn't get out of bed and even my father could see there was something the matter with me. Mrs. Jones took my temperature.

"104! Indeed to goodness!" she cried, wiping my hot face with a flannel. "It's Dr Idris-Jones we'll be sending for."

Dr Idris-Jones was so fat he could hardly squeeze through the door of my room. When he bent over my bed and began prodding my tummy, I was convinced I was about to be smothered by this vast grey-and-white pin-striped balloon that kept fading and looming over me. Was this to be my punishment for losing my forty pound plate? It seemed quite possible.

"Acute appendicitis it is," I heard him say in his funny sing-song voice. "This child must be operated on at once."

For the first time in my life I felt sorry for my father when I saw his face. I remembered that his brother, my Uncle Cedric, had died of appendicitis when he was about my age.

I didn't usually think about dying, but I thought about it as I was being bundled up in blankets and carried downstairs to the car.

Peter Pan said, "To die would be a very great adventure." I hoped he was right.

My father came to see me every one of the ten days I was in hospital. I gradually lost a little of my awe of him as he sat patiently by my bed teaching me to play Whist when I knew he'd much rather be out on *Sea Scout*.

Waiting for him to come striding into my room in his grey flannels, the sleeves of his open-necked white shirt rolled back from his hairy sun-tanned arms, I allowed myself, tentatively and secretly, to begin to love him.

My experience of love so far was limited to the anxious and protective love I felt for Thomas and my devotion to the horses and dogs. It seemed safer to keep this new love to myself. For one thing, I wasn't sure my father would *want* me to love him. My sister Iris had wanted to love him, and she'd been sent away to boarding school. You just never knew with grown-ups.

My room was on the ground floor of the little cottage hospital and the window beside my bed opened onto a dusty, un-paved street. The local children soon discovered that my father brought me presents every day. As if by magic, they appeared at my window as soon as he left. Ragged, barefoot, speaking a language I couldn't make any sense of, they thrust their grubby hands over the window-sill, waiting for me to share my Rollos and cherries and copies of Beano and Dandy comics with them. They reminded me of Our-Edly and his gang. They were company of a sort, and a comfort in a strange place.

When my mother arrived in Wales with the rest of the family she said to my father, "I expect you terrorized the poor child over losing that wretched plate and made her have appendicitis."

My father looked so guilt-stricken that when I was well again I tried for his sake to learn to love *Sea Scout*. I didn't succeed, but I did try.

My teeth stayed crooked till my husband had them straightened for me eight years later as a twentieth birthday present.

But not even appendicitis or horrible *Sea Scout* could spoil the bliss of those weeks by the sea; hard ribbed sand under paddling feet, sweet donkeys in straw hats to ride along the beach, rocks to climb, shells to collect, tidal pools to poke about in. There always seemed to be an Italian ice cream vendor driving a brightly-painted horse-drawn cart, and a Hurdy-Gurdy Man turning the handle of his barrel organ: *Daisy, Daisy, give me your answer dooo, I'm half crazy all for the love of youooo....* Often there'd be a little monkey in a red cap and jacket to collect our pennies in the Hurdy-Gurdy Man's hat.

Sometimes a Punch and Judy Show arrived, and I'd join the small audience of children sitting on the sand in front of the striped canvas booth,

half repelled, half fascinated by beastly Punch abusing poor Judy. I imagine they'd be banned today, though children see ten times worse on television.

But far and away the best thing about those summer holidays by the sea was the sand. How I loved the sand! I loved building with it, digging in it, burrowing in it, rolling in it. It got everywhere: In our canvas shoes, in our picnic sandwiches, sagging in the seats of our wet woolen bathing suits, in our beds, stuck to our scalps, in little trails and

Me with a friend on the beach

heaps on the sun-bleached floors of our temporary homes.

Even Nanny couldn't discipline the sand.

Christmas was the other welcome break in the monotony of nursery life. The count-down began in November with an invitation from the cook to the entire household to stir silver charms into the Christmas pudding mixture and make a wish. Every year I wished for an Arab stallion.

"If you tell your wish it won't come true," cautioned Ivy. I hoped she had better luck with her wishes than I did. (Though oddly enough, many years later my wish was granted, and for a whole summer I cantered a beautiful Arab stallion called Lahiff along a beach each evening as the sun set over the sea on the Greek island of Skiathos.)

The poor quality of war-time paper and watercolour meant that our home-made Christmas cards came out disappointingly wrinkled and anemic; Father Christmas clad in pink. Pink robins. But if they didn't sway and fall into the drawing room fire they held pride of place on the mantelpiece among the ranks of stiff cards with addresses printed inside and Charles and Barbara Farthingale crossed out and Charlie and Babs written in by hand. Soon we were forbidden to look on the top shelf of the linen cupboard, where we naturally kept a close eye on the growing pile of presents in their tinsel wrappings.

Every room in the house was occupied at Christmas. Suitcases were unpacked amid clouds of tissue paper, the maids scurried up and down stairs answering bells, carrying freshly pressed dresses, more coal for bedroom fires, vases of hot-house flowers. Rich smells drifted from the kitchen. Nursery rules were relaxed a little.

"Darling! Come here and let me look at you! Goodness how you've grown! Pascoe, just look how this child's shot up!"

Why did grown-ups always say that? Didn't children usually grow? How else would they get to be grown-ups? Actually, I wasn't sure I wanted to be a grown-up. Not if it meant wearing a corset like Aunty Nini's, or having to sleep in the same bed with someone like my father's friend Mouse.

Among the regular Christmas visitors were Granny Ting and Grandpa Hayward, various aunts and uncles, tweedy, red-faced Mouse, my mother's limp-wristed friend Dizzy, (a young man whose shrill laugh and mincing walk made my father grind his teeth), and Thomas's godfather, Fuzzy, who was spectacularly bald.

"It's rude to stare," said Nanny. How could you not stare when a fly alighted on that polished pink dome?

When Nanny brought us down to the drawing room after tea on Christmas Eve everyone made a fuss of us the way grown-ups do when they're showing other grown-ups how good they are with children.

Every now and then one of them would raise a finger and say "Listen!" In the ensuing silence they'd say, "Funny! I could have sworn I heard bells!" Then they'd look at us children and smile at each other and go back to sipping their cocktails and talking among themselves.

But I knew that somewhere out there in the thrilling darkness Father Christmas's sleigh was streaming through the sky, whip cracking, reindeer prancing and tossing their jingling harness, *heading straight for our house!*

He never rang the front door bell like ordinary visitors. Not he! Not Father Christmas! He banged on the door with his fist, making the dogs bark and freezing us children in an agony of delicious terror. My father would put his cocktail glass down and stride out into the hall and fling open the front door and the hall was filled with the splendid scarlet presence, gusty roars of laughter, the stamp of big black boots: the incarnation of Christmas.

The grown-ups trooped out of the drawing room and gathered near the sparkling Christmas tree and Johnny and I, pressing close for mutual courage, awaited the dreaded moment when Father Christmas would boom, "Well, Nanny, have these children been good this year?"

Pin-drop silence. Was Nanny going to tell about the sewing-up of Uncle Pascoe's pajama legs? The near-execution of Our-Edly? The accidental setting fire to the nursery curtains? I'd be quite blue in the face with holding my breath by the time she said grudgingly: "Well, Father Christmas, I dare say they could have been worse." Saved! All that remained now was to whisper our hopes concerning presents into Father Christmas's ear and stumble through the carol we'd been rehearsing for the occasion.

Well, Nanny, have these children been good this year?

Such was our relief that Nanny hadn't betrayed us that we didn't even hear the time when Granny Ting, merry on a glass of Bristol Cream, apparently remarked, "Doesn't Herbert make a splendid Father Christmas?"

Later in the night nursery, one of our father's long woolly shooting stockings pinned to the end of each of our beds, I'd whisper to Johnny, "Are you asleep yet?"

"No," he'd whisper fiercely, "but shut up, I'm *trying*." Everyone knew that Father Christmas didn't come if you weren't asleep. Suppose you couldn't go to sleep *all night*?

From the moment we opened our eyes to see those limp stockings promisingly lumpy and bulgy in the freezing grey dawn, nothing about Christmas was ever a disappointment. I didn't even mind church for once because I loved the carols, and the crèche set up by the font. And while the vicar droned on I could think about the presents I'd received, and the crackers and paper hats at lunch, and the Christmas cake at tea time, its crunchy white icing decorated with tiny silver balls and reindeer and skiers and fir trees.

On Christmas afternoon the servants had their own party in the huge stone-floored laundry room off the kitchen. The main entertainment—famous throughout the village—was a one-man show written and produced by Herbert, starring Herbert, and featuring rude "pomes" and ditties poking disrespectful fun at his employers. Once Johnny overheard Herbert trying out one of his jokes on Fairfax the head gardener and he repeated it to me. It went like this: "I missed my chance last week, and no mistake! I was having a bit of trouble hanging a new picture over the bed in the master bedroom when in comes the mistress and she says to me—I do not tell a lie—she says, 'Herbert, if we get on the bed together and I give you a bit of help we'll soon get it up'."

Johnny and I stared at each other. What was funny about that? Was he sure he'd got it right? Johnny insisted he had. Later in the afternoon we could hear the shrieks of laughter from the laundry room all the way up in the nursery.

My parents provided unlimited food and beer for the party, and for once my mother didn't say anything if the cocktail tray arrived late or Ivy, her cap a little askew, tripped over the rug on her way out of the drawing room.

On Boxing Day we were taken to the Pantomime in Nottingham. We always sat in the middle of the front row of the Dress Circle, and during the intermission we had ice creams in tubs with little wooden spoons that made my tongue curl up. Our mother and Nanny had tea and biscuits on trays.

Remembering that electrifying moment when the lights dimmed and the chattering and rustling of the audience died away and the orchestra struck up the Overture, I wonder if modern children, sated with television and movies and video games, can ever know such breathless anticipation? And when the great red velvet curtains swooped back to reveal a brilliantly lit fairy-tale world of people and animals sprung suddenly into dancing singing life—surely that was the nearest thing to pure magic a small child could ever experience.

Of course there are still pantomimes of a sort being staged at Christmas, but in those days the pantomime still belonged to its rightful audience— the children. The Principle Boy was played by a rollicking girl in tights and high heels, not some male pop star, and the role of the Dame was taken by an elderly male actor whose antics made us laugh till we fell out of our seats. We sang *Ten Green Bottles* and *The Smoke Goes Up The Chimney Just The Same*, and made the gilded rafters ring with our boos and hisses and shrieks of warning when the dragon or the wicked uncle crept up on the unsuspecting lovers.

Genies leaping from puffs of smoke, Cinderella waltzing at the Ball with her Prince, Dick Whittington's cat stalking along the Dress Circle barrier during the Intermission, good overcoming evil, happy-ever-after endings—I would hug it all to myself as we left the theatre, hoping that no one would speak to me and break the spell.

"Did you enjoy it, darling?" my mother was bound to ask as soon as we were in the car. "The cat's got her tongue," said Nanny.

As Herbert drove us home through the freezing night to the prospect of a special supper of poached eggs on toast by the nursery fire I drew the fur rug up to my nose and gazed out of the window at the streaming darkness, re-living and storing away every moment, saturated in bliss.

Later, eating my egg and watching the firelight, I'd come reluctantly back to earth, comforted by the knowledge that it would all happen again next year; unchanging, perfect.

I didn't know then that nothing lasts for ever.

Chapter 10

The Pied Piper of Edwinstowe

Sir William was to be our family's catalyst. Nothing would ever be the same after the winter's night when he came swashbuckling over the front doorstep.

My father brought him home for dinner shortly after the beginning of the war, and he ended up more or less living with us for six years till it ended. Eventually, like some irresistible Pied Piper, he would lead my parents off to live in South Africa.

I was sitting on the tumpty in front of the drawing room fire in my dressing gown eating bread-and-milk out of a big blue breakfast cup the first time Sir William came to Edwinstowe. My mother was reading to me. I already knew the book by heart, but she didn't know that, and having her read to me and being allowed to have supper in the drawing room were rare treats. Bread-and-milk was my favourite supper; crunchy with sugar on the top, the square chunks of bread swollen with hot milk. The crusty bits were best. I saved them till last. The book was '*The Story of Heather.*' I always cried when Trixie fell into the bog and was sucked under by the mud. Heather and Trixie were Exmoor ponies.

My mother was wearing her clingy scarlet evening dress. It licked up her body like a flame. A single strand of pearls lay round her throat, a tiny heart of firelight reflected in each pearl.

We heard the crunch of gravel outside and car doors slamming.

My mother looked up, closing the book. "Here comes your father," she said. Soon he would come in bringing other worlds and the cold dark night into the circle of firelight and bend over her chair and kiss her. Then he would mix them both a cocktail. Then he'd go upstairs and change into his dinner jacket, which would have been laid out for him in his dressing room by Violet. That was the evening ritual.

My father's gun dogs, Dinky the Cocker spaniel and a black Labrador called Dash, had been dreaming and twitching by the fire. They leaped up at the sound of the car and tore into the hall barking and runkling the rugs, their claws scrabbling on the flagstone floor. The front door opened and banged shut and a rush of cold air came down the hall and into the drawing room, jostling the flames in the fireplace.

"Get *down*, boys!" I heard my father order.

The dogs came wagging back into the room escorting my father and a tall, broad-shouldered stranger. Whereas my father's grayish hair was thinning and close-cropped, the stranger's hair was thick and silver, combed straight back and falling in curls on the collar of his dark suit. It gave him the look of a buccaneer.

"Darling," said my father, "this is Sir William Firth. I do hope dinner will stretch?"

Sir William advanced across the drawing room and bent to take the hand my mother held out to him. I watched her with interest. I hadn't known before that grown-ups blushed.

"And this is Diana," said my mother.

I put down my cup of bread and milk and scrambled to my feet. Sir William looked down at me as if he was really seeing me and shook my hand as if I was a grown-up and said, "How do you do, Diana?" He had deep-set brown eyes and he looked as if he was about to tell you a wonderful joke.

There was a strange, still tension in the room, just like before a thunder storm. The electricity in the air was making the little hairs on my arms and the back of my neck stand up.

In no time Sir William, or Will as he rapidly became to my parents, was installed in one of the spare bedrooms. He spent the week nights at Edwinstowe and returned to his wife and home in Sussex at weekends.

At first his chauffeur stayed at Edwinstowe too—apparently Sir William had never learned to drive—but soon his services were no longer required.

My mother was to be seen each morning behind the wheel of one of Sir William's various Rolls Royces, driving gaily off to take him to his meetings and appointments. When summer came, the wicker picnic basket and a rug were often on the back seat. Sir William loved picnics and my mother, previously famous for complaining about sand or ants, suddenly loved picnics too.

The entire household fell under Sir William's spell. My father brought his precious Taylor '21 port up from the cellar to drink with him as they lingered at the dining room table late into the night, winning the war and solving the world's problems. ("Keeping the servants up," my mother complained.) Herbert never grumbled about the extra cars to look after or shoes to polish and the maids grew pink and flustered and dropped things when he spoke to them. Even Nanny couldn't be cross with him for long, though she saw her authority in the nursery constantly undermined.

A titan of industry Sir William may have been, but his sense of fun and dazzling disregard for the rules kept us children in a constant state of what Nanny called disapprovingly "Over-excitement."

One day he stole the butcher boy's bicycle from outside the back door and went weaving off down the village street with two-year-old Thomas screaming with excitement in the big basket on the handlebars. He smuggled food up to the loft and joined us for midnight feasts and ghost stories, poured a whole packet of precious rationed Lux soap flakes into the bath to make us a bubble bath, and took us to unsuitable films at the village cinema which give me nightmares that kept Nanny up half the night.

Caught red-handed conducting a wild game of somersaults off the high headboards of our beds at bedtime one evening, he seized Nanny round her stout waist and waltzed her round the room and toppled her, legs in the air, long navy knickers in full view, dignity in ruins, onto one of the beds.

"Don't be cross, Nanny darling," he said, setting her back on her feet and straightening her cap and bending to kiss her downy cheek.

. . . waltzed her around the room, and toppled her,
legs in the air, long navy knickers in full view,
dignity in ruins, onto one of the beds

Johnny and I waited, round-eyed, for the full majesty of Nanny's wrath to descend on Sir William's unsuspecting head. We held our breath as she frowned at him and marshaled her large bosom back into its rightful place. Sir William watched her, his head on one side, his eyes gleaming. Then, to our utter amazement, her lips began to twitch and her chins began to wobble *and she burst out laughing!*

"Sir William, Sir William!" she exclaimed, shooing him tenderly towards the door, "you'll be the death of me yet!"

It was also Sir William who showed Johnny how to make the primitive periscope we took up onto the roof outside the maids' bathroom one summer afternoon to spy on the maids having their baths.

"What can you see?" I whispered, spread-eagled below Johnny.

The roof was steep and slippery and the hot slates were burning my hands and bare knees. I was trying not to look down.

"It's Ivy," Johnny reported. "She's taking off her dressing gown and putting it on a chair. She's got a spotty botty." He spluttered with mirth and I giggled and slid down the roof a bit.

"She's getting in the bath now," said Johnny. "She's turning round to sit down. I say! She's got *hair!*"

"Well I know *that*," I said, disappointed.

"No, stupid. Between her legs."

Between her *legs*? Poor Ivy, how terrible for her! I vowed to be specially nice to her in future.

Sir William was always giving us all the most marvelous presents. At Christmas he gave my mother a mink coat, followed by one of his Rolls Royces for her birthday. Both gifts—perhaps understandably—incurred disapproving lectures from my father. So for her next birthday, having discovered that she collected six-sided threepenny pieces in a drawer in her desk, Sir William had five hundred pounds in threepenny pieces delivered to my parents' suite at the Savoy. The huge number of heavy sacks of coins must have caused quite a commotion in the lobby, (and of course they all had to be returned to the bank), and the manager can't have been at all pleased. But I expect Sir William stuffed big white five pound notes in his pockets and said, "Don't be cross, darling," and remained one of his favourite guests.

Sir William called everyone darling. My father. Nanny. Taxi drivers. The King, for all I knew.

"This has got to stop, Will!" roared my father one day when he came out of his study to find himself engulfed in a fluttering scurrying squawking storm of feathers and fur.

Herbert had just carried several dark green Harrods boxes in from the Rolls, and Thomas, who was probably about four at the time, was excitedly tearing the lids off and releasing pairs of rabbits and hamsters and guinea pigs and bantams and feathery-footed pigeons all over the hall. My father should have been glad that Harrods didn't stock alligators or pythons at the time.

"It's his birthday, darling," said Sir William—rightly guessing that our father had no idea when Thomas's birthday was.

Predictably enough, Thomas soon got bored with the care and feeding of all these creatures, and the job fell to me. Of the whole menagerie, only Cocky, the brilliantly feathered little bantam cockerel, became an interesting character; a rock star among bantams. Declining to live in a pen with his small, dull, governess-coloured mate, he patrolled the grounds, attempting to impress the dogs and gardeners with

Johnny, 14, Thomas, 4, and me, 12

aggressively macho displays. He trailed stiffened wings along the ground, the bunch of feathers on his head tossing like Rod Stewart's hair, and flashed his lethal-looking spurs at alarmed visitors.

It was all for show; Cocky was a big fraud. Secretly he liked nothing better than to be wrapped in a shawl and tucked up in the old doll's pram for a nap or, in cold weather, to be allowed to sit on a warm spot on the back of the Aga cooker in the kitchen. He had one spectacular party trick, saved to impress people who had never met him before. I'd be holding him and scratching him behind his splendid crest of iridescent head feathers when suddenly, without any warning, he'd slump dramatically over my arm and dangle head-down, inert and motionless and apparently dead. When he felt he'd caused enough of a sensation he would make a miraculous recovery and right himself and all but take a bow.

Poor Cocky, after many years he disappeared one night, victim—it was feared—of a fox who wasn't fooled by his swagger and bravado.

I was about twelve when Sir William took me home with him to Sussex for the weekend for the first time. He lived in a rambling stone house with a moat and drawbridge. There were a lot of daunting servants who never smiled gliding about silently as if on wheels and suddenly appearing and making me jump. An eerie hush waited in the long shadowy corridors and gloomy rooms. Everywhere there were heavy swathes of tasseled and fringed curtains just right for burglars or madmen with axes to hide behind and, unlike at Edwinstowe, you just knew the diamond-leaded casement windows were never opened. There were no dogs. Not even a cat. No wonder Sir William liked it so much at Edwinstowe.

Sir William's wife Lena was supposed to have been a renowned theatrical beauty in her youth, but you'd never have known. She had complicated, very black hair and a disagreeable expression and spent the entire weekend lying on a sofa in the drawing room eating about a year's ration of chocolates from Fortnum & Mason and reading *The Tatler*.

The only things she said to me the whole weekend were, "My dear friend the Countess of Davisport is in *The Tatler* this week" and, "Is it true your mother has been *divorced*?"

There was always so much to do when you were with Sir William. We rowed round the moat in a rotting boat and tried to catch the carp lurking under the drawbridge. We fed the peacocks who strutted on the shaven lawns by day and screamed from the treetops at night, jerking me awake among the musty curtains of my four-masted galleon of a bed. We dismantled a suit of armour in the hall to see if it would fit me, and when we couldn't put it back together again we hid it from Lena in a cupboard. One afternoon we built a magnificent bonfire. Sir William put his head in at the drawing room window and said to Lena, "Darling! Do come out and see our bonfire!"

"No thank you," snapped Lena, "I can see quite enough of it from here. Your hat is on fire."

But best of all was Patsy, the tall bay mare Sir William hired for me to ride on Saturday afternoon. He didn't ride himself, claiming that horses were "dangerous at both ends and rude at one." I couldn't wait to repeat that to Johnny.

Sitting beside Sir William in the back of the car on the way home to Edwinstowe after the most satisfactory and action-packed weekend of my life so far, I gazed out of the window and watched cloud shadows chase each other over the hills and remembered how Patsy and I had flown just as effortlessly across the fields and over the tallest fence I'd ever jumped in my life.

"You're very quiet," said Sir William, "what are you thinking about?"

"Riding Patsy," I said.

"Ah. You liked her, didn't you?"

"Liked her? Oh, she was—she was *perfect*," I said inadequately.

"Ah," said Sir William again. Then he opened his newspaper and left me to dream in peace.

The thing was that much as I loved Beauty, and much as I would never dream of being disloyal to her, I had grown so tall lately that my feet nearly touched the ground now when I rode her.

"I don't 'alf feel sorry for that poor bleedin' 'orse." jeered Our-Edly as I rode through the village the previous week, convulsing his lieutenants, who nearly fell off the fence where they were sitting in a row smoking cigarettes they had probably stolen from Mrs. Grundy's shop.

The week after my stay with Sir William, Ivy came into the drawing room with a telegram on a silver salver. My father picked it up and glanced at it.

"It's for you," he said, handing it to me.

For me? Even Johnny had never received a telegram! I tore open the orange envelope and read the cryptic ticker-tape message: *Meet the 2.25 train on Thursday.* It was unsigned.

Arriving far too early on the station platform the next day, I had to wait for the train for what seemed an eternity among the milk churns and rustling baskets of racing pigeons.

Jim-the-porter was watering the geraniums. He winked at me in my childish shorts and sandals and said, "Come to meet yer young man then, 'ave yer?"

At last the train appeared and came rushing along the platform as if it had no intention of stopping at such an insignificant little station. Changing its mind at the last moment, it jolted to a halt, hissing and steaming, and disgorged a few passengers onto the platform. They hurried off and doors slammed and the Guard blew his whistle and waved his red flag.

The train jerked forward. Even though I'd had no idea what to expect, I was stunned with anti-climax.

Slouching towards the exit, I paused to watch the Station Master helping Jim-the-porter unbolt and drop the side of a cattle truck which must have been detached from the back of the train. Jim-the-porter clambered up the ramp and disappeared inside. I was about to turn away when there was a sudden rattle of hooves and a terrified horse came plunging down the ramp, an equally terrified Jim-the-porter swinging and cursing on the end of its halter. I thought my heart would burst with joy when I realized that the wild creature lashing out at the Station Master's waving arms was—*Patsy*!

"Sign here," said the Station Master.

"You can have 'er and welcome," said Jim-the-porter, handing me her halter.

Still frightened after her journey, trembling and prancing and shying at every leaf or scrap of paper fluttering in a gutter, Patsy nearly pulled me off my feet several times on the way home.

When we clattered into the stable yard Cartledge was hosing down the cobblestones.

"What's this then?" he asked.

Me with Patsy

"Her name is Patsy. I think she's a present. From Sir William."

"A present, eh?" He ran an expert hand down her legs and stood back, head on one side, looking her over. "Nice bit of horseflesh," he said judiciously.

A nice bit of horseflesh? But I knew that from Cartledge this was high praise.

"Get some straw and rub her down. She's dripping wet," he said, going back to his hosing.

As I led her into the stables Actress neighed a friendly welcome and Beauty put her head out of her loose box and bit Patsy's neck, letting her know who was going to be boss.

As a final, perfect gesture, Sir William had even thought to buy Patsy's saddle and bridle for me. When they were delivered to the house later that evening, I burst into tears.

"Over excited," said Nanny. "Early to bed for you."

For a few days I lived in fear that I wouldn't be allowed to keep my beautiful horse. But nothing was said, and the following week a big black motor bike arrived, just in time for Johnny's fifteenth birthday.

Sir William made no bones about the fact that he came from very humble beginnings. He told us he had left school when he was nine and delivered newspapers and collected scrap metal in a wheelbarrow to help support his family. Born "within the sound of Bow Bells" in London, he still retained faint traces of a Cockney accent.

"Sir William is one of nature's gentlemen," I'd heard my mother say.

"Is Sir William privileged?" I asked her one day as I was watching her arrange a bowl of sweet-peas for his room. I'd never satisfactorily resolved the question—which Sir William himself had raised—about what it meant to be privileged.

"Whatever do you mean, darling?"

"Well, is he as privileged as us?"

"Do you mean is he as wealthy as us? You know it's very bad manners to talk about money, darling."

But it wasn't money I was talking about. I was fumbling my way towards the mysteries of *class.*

Sir William's childhood sounded as if it had been more like Our-Edly's than Johnny's and mine, but I didn't think Our-Edly would ever become a gentleman. Not even one of nature's sort.

Chapter 11

Uprooted

My father seemed to be grumpier than usual. Even the dogs were keeping out of his way. You'd have thought he'd be glad the war was over and there'd be no more people being killed or Doodle Bugs and V2 rockets raining down on London. But it seemed the fury he'd directed at Hitler for the last six years was now being leveled nearer home. At the British people, in fact.

"Ungrateful bloody lot," he roared when we heard on the wireless that Winston Churchill had been voted out of office in the General Election, replaced by Clement Atlee and his Labour government. Raised as I'd been on broadcasts of Mr. Churchill's stirring speeches on the wireless and newspaper pictures of his defiant figure striding through the ruins of London, a cigar clamped in his jaws, two fingers raised in his V for Victory sign, Mr. Atlee certainly seemed a poor substitute. He looked exactly like a Beatrix Potter mouse in a little black jacket.

Now the war was over it seemed that Sir William wouldn't be living with us any more. One day his chauffeur arrived and piled his luggage into the back of the Rolls and drove him away. We were all sad to see him go, but to look at my mother you'd think Hitler had won the war.

As if Sir William's departure wasn't enough of a blow to her, the next thing was that the current governess handed in her notice. And governesses, like domestic servants, were fast becoming a vanishing breed.

Apparently the governess had been drawing the nursery curtains after tea when Houdini, Thomas's missing hamster, fell off the pelmet and landed on her head. She'd been sewing, and Houdini gave her such a fright she swallowed some pins she was holding between her lips.

"I should eat a piece of bread if I were you," advised my mother, "I'm sure you'll be quite all right."

But we never knew if she was all right or not because the next day she packed her bags and had herself driven away in the village taxi.

A few days later my mother sent for me in the drawing room and said, "Your father and I have decided it is time for you to go boarding school."

"But I don't want to go to boarding school!"

"Nonsense," said my mother, "you'll love it. Games and friends and things," she added vaguely.

"I'm sorry about Houdini," I said, but I sensed that it was hopeless. My fate had already been sealed. Sometimes being a child is like one of those nightmares where something is chasing you and you can't run because your legs are being sucked down in a bog just like Trixie the Exmoor pony.

This nightmare got much worse.

The phone had been ringing a lot lately and the telegram boy had been peddling up the drive with his black satchel over his shoulder more often than usual. He always seemed to be hanging around the back door, making the scullery maid blush and giggle while he waited for a reply.

Something was afoot, but even the maids' sitting room—usually such a reliable source of information—was no help. Then on Thursday afternoon Twizzy-Lizzy the hairdresser arrived, bursting with important news.

"Well," she said, lighting the little blue flame under her curling tongs, "I hear you'll all soon be off down South. Rather you than me, I must say."

A gratifying silence greeted this announcement.

"*Down South?*" chorused Violet and Ivy.

"Ay," said Twizzy-Lizzy, "it's all over the village. His Nibs has got some important new job in London. On the National Coal Board. They'll soon be flitting, you mark my words."

(My Norwegian sister-in-law told me recently that *flytte* is the Norwegian verb *to move*. A word left behind in our part of the world by long-ago Norse invaders.)

Under the table where I was sitting, I counted the row of bobbles along a fold in the green table cloth. If there was a seven in the number it wasn't true that we were leaving Edwinstowe. Sixteen. I moved the fold a little to make it seventeen, although I knew it didn't count if you cheated.

I slipped out of the sitting room unnoticed in the pandemonium caused by Twizzly-Lizzy's bombshell and went to find my mother.

"Is it true we're going to flit?"

"Darling, where do you pick up words like that? So common."

"Twizzly-Lizzy says we're leaving Edwinstowe!"

My mother sighed. "Oh dear, this village. It's like living in a goldfish bowl. It'll be a blessing to get away from the endless gossip."

"It's true then?"

My mother was tidying the bottom drawer of her desk, which she always kept locked. According to Johnny it was full of love letters. She said, "Mr. Atlee has offered your father a very important job in London."

"But he *hates* Mr. Atlee! He says he's a bloody socialist!"

"Don't use that word, darling."

"What, socialist?"

"No. The—other one. It's a great honour for your father. His country needs him," she added in a proud, soppy voice.

"But we can't leave Edwinstowe! We live here! We've always lived here! This is our *home*!"

"But darling, it's just a house. And Sir William has already found us a nice new house. Quite near where he lives, as it happens. Won't that be lovely?"

That explained why she'd been looking cheerful lately. She closed the desk drawer and locked it and stood up and gave me an unexpected hug.

"Cheer up, darling," she said, "your father is going to sell Actress, but he says you can take your horses to Surrey."

We might not have taken them?

My mother was humming and fluffing her hair in the mirror over the desk. I ran upstairs to the nursery. Nanny was sitting by the fire surrounded by Peter Jones boxes full of my new school uniform, stitching Cashes' name-tapes on piles of hankies and socks and knickers. I ran back downstairs. Dusk was falling as I crossed the yard to the stables. Inside it was warm and steamy and smelt comfortingly of straw and leather and saddle-soap and manure. Patsy was munching hay in her loose-box, snatching mouthfuls down from the hay-rack above her head. I put my face against her coarse brown mane and burst into tears.

I heard Cartledge slide back the bolt and come in, accompanied by a mealy whiff of bran mash. The horses always had bran mash and molasses for supper on Fridays. How easily you take small familiar things like bran mash on Fridays for granted till they stop happening. *What will take the place of everything I know?*

"Now then, what's this?" said Cartledge. But I could tell from his voice that he'd already heard.

The handle of the metal bucket clanked as he put it down in the straw. I felt his hands on my shoulders. He turned me round and dried my eyes and blew my nose with his handkerchief the way he used to when I fell off Beauty when I was learning to jump. I was taller than him now. He held me awkwardly and patted my back.

"There there," he kept saying "there there." What else was there to say?

"Not a bleedin' thing," Our-Edly would have said if you'd asked him.

I was told that my new school was in Buckinghamshire.

"Very pretty countryside, I believe," my mother said. "Barbara Wright's daughter goes there, and she absolutely *adores* it."

I didn't even know Barbara Wright or her daughter, but they were being allowed to decide my fate? My parents obviously hadn't even bothered to go and look at the place.

I rode my familiar forest trails and visited my secret haunts for the last time. Mist rose from the dying bracken and wreathed the branches of the oak trees. Rows of rain drops trembled on every twig. Patsy's breath steamed and her hoof beats were muffled by sodden leaves.

Inside the Major Oak I listened for Robin and his men, but all I could hear was the sound of my own breathing and rain pattering on dead leaves outside.

On the way home through the village I stopped to say goodbye to Mr. Bostock and the Blacksmith and Mrs. Grundy. Mr. Bostock shook my hand vigorously and wished me "all the best" and gave me a packet of Smith's Crisps. The Blacksmith selected an old shoe from the pile at the back of the forge and wiped it on his leather apron and gave it to me for luck. Mrs. Grundy gave me a whiskery kiss and a packet of Licorice Allsorts and said, "Don't forget us, my duck."

"Go to hell!" her parrot shouted after me like a prophet of doom as I left the shop.

Our-Edly was bouncing a ball against the doors of the stable yard when I rode up and dismounted. I glanced round, alert for a trap of some kind, but he appeared to be alone.

"Leavin', then, are yer?" he said

"Yes."

"Won't be comin' back no more?"

"No."

"Well, terrah then."

"Goodbye."

He hesitated, glancing around just as I had. Then he fumbled in his pocket and held out his hand. "Yer might as well 'ave this."

He gave me an enormous horse-chestnut. It must have been the prize of his conker collection.

"Gosh, thanks." I gave him half my Licorice Allsorts.

He wouldn't look at me. He slouched off, bouncing his ball on the road, tossing one last "Tarrah," over his shoulder.

I took Patsy into her stable and unsaddled her and gave her and Beauty and Actress a few Licorice Allsorts. Then I went round to have tea at Nanny's house.

Sitting on the rag rug at Bear's feet, the heat from the range roasting my face, I burst out, "I don't want to *go!*" I was trying hard not to cry.

Our-Edly . . . fumbled in his pocket and held out his hand.
"Yer might as well 'ave this"

I felt Bear's hand against my hot cheek. "Eh, lass, don't thee fret," he said. "It'll all work out for t' best. He's a fine man, is your father. We're going to need him down there in London looking out for us all with this new-fangled Nationalization caper."

It was only later that I would come to understand that my father, Conservative to the core, was violently opposed to the Labour government's nationalization policy, and at first had rejected with characteristic bluntness all overtures from the Prime Minister to join the National Coal Board. Then, when he saw that it was to be composed almost entirely of politicians who didn't know the first thing about coal mining, he changed his mind and accepted the appointment of Production Director. He hoped—in vain, as it turned out—that he would be able to influence policy and protect the industry in which he had worked all his life.

Nanny and Bear gave me my favourite Coronation mug off the mantle when I said goodbye to them, but it disappeared in the move. My mother seemed to think it might have been broken. She couldn't understand why I was upset. She said it was only a cheap souvenir.

Chapter 12

Banished

It was raining heavily as the Rolls entered a dark tunnel of giant rhododendron bushes leading to my boarding school. Their twisted, slimy-looking limbs reminded me of the cartoon forest Snow White fled through to escape her wicked step-mother. A great dark crenellated building loomed out of the downpour as the Rolls drew to a halt.

I was dressed in my itchy school uniform and hideous felt hat with the elastic cutting into my chin. Herbert deposited me under a massive portico with my trunk and rang the front door bell. When we heard footsteps approaching he touched his cap and said, "Good luck, Miss." I held out my hand and he shook it. Then he splashed back through the puddles and got into the Rolls and drove off.

I'd arrived after the term had started and the other "new bugs" had already found their way around the labyrinth of passages and knew what lay behind the dozens of identical doors and had paired off with "best friends."

They'd also had a chance to learn the rules, many of which—like only prefects being allowed to use the main staircase—were unwritten.

"You! What's your name?"

"Diana Young."

"Who do you think you are? Come back down here and go and use the back stairs! And think yourself lucky. If I catch you again you'll get an Order Mark!"

If you've never been away from home before, never slept in a dormitory, never bathed, (twice a week, having found your name on the bath list), and brushed your teeth and dressed and undressed in public, never had to leap up and rush off somewhere with a pushing shouting thundering herd of other girls every time a bell rang, it's not easy to get used to it. The only place you could ever be by yourself was in one of the row of smelly lavatories, and even there the doors had big gaps above and below, excluding any real privacy. There were squares of newspaper threaded on string instead of normal paper, and usually someone banging on the door and rattling the handle shouting, "Wind up, whoever's in there!"

Tall for my age, and hopelessly backward, I was put in a form with much younger girls. I towered over them like Gulliver but I still couldn't do the lessons. Gym and games were no better. For some reason I seemed incapable of climbing a rope or running and bouncing with a great *thud* on the springboard and soaring over the leather "horse." Out on the bitter, windswept playing fields the games mistress was always blowing her whistle and yelling "No Diana! The other way!" as I ran stumbling over the hummocky grass or threw the ball in the wrong direction in lacrosse or netball. No one wanted me on their team, and who could blame them?

Mealtimes were another nightmare. A maid would bang a plate down in front of me with—for example—a greasy rolled-up lump of grey suet spotted with a few currants, sweating in a pool of congealed custard.

"What's this?" I asked my neighbour.

"Dead man's leg," she said. "I'll have yours if you don't want it."

The dormitory where I slept was furnished with two rows of narrow iron beds with thin mattresses, six along each wall, separated from each other by shabby chests-of-drawers. There were no curtains and no rugs on the rough wood floor. You were allowed to have three personal items on your chest-of-drawers. Most girls had silver or leather-framed photos of their parents, either soft-focus studio portraits or enlarged snapshots of them got up in tiaras and white ties or on hunters or yachts or skis. These photos were closely scrutinized. I had only brought my almost hairless teddy-bear and Our-Edly's conker and the horseshoe the blacksmith had given me. I expect my lack of photos was held against me.

At first I couldn't think what the dormitory reminded me of. Then I realized that its bare boards and icy drafts and battered furniture and single dim light bulb dangling from the cracked ceiling was like the maids' bedroom I'd seen once at Edwinstowe.

I was too young then to appreciate the irony of my parents paying handsomely to house their daughter in the same wretched conditions as their servants.

At bedtime one of the mistresses would put her head round the dormitory door and say: "Goodnight, girls. No talking after lights out!" and plunge the room into whispering giggling darkness.

I cried myself to sleep most nights, shivering under a threadbare blanket because you were supposed to bring your own eiderdown from home.

It was strange to feel so lonely, surrounded by more girls of my own age than I'd met in my whole life. But I was far too shy to speak to anyone, and hardly anyone ever spoke to me except to say things like "Pass the sugar" or "You can't sit there. I'm saving that chair for Samantha."

Never having had a friend before, I didn't know how to go about getting one. Once I plucked up my courage and went up to a chattering group during break. I'd seen one of them drop an envelope while we were waiting in the queue for our eleven o'clock mugs of watery cocoa and stale currant buns. They nudged each other and fell silent as I approached.

"Oh, thanks," said the girl when I handed her the envelope. I hesitated, and they all stared coldly at me till I turned and walked away.

"There goes Popocatepetl," one of them said. There was a burst of laughter and someone else said, "Oh you are awful, Katie!"

I looked up Popocatepetl in the Encyclopedia in the library. It was a seventeen thousand foot high volcano in Mexico.

Sundays were another source of humiliation. You needed someone to walk with in the two-by-two crocodile to the village church. "Come along, dear. You can walk with me," the mistress who accompanied us would say when it was time to set out.

When letters from home were given out by one of the Prefects after supper, some lucky girls sometimes got two or three.

"Are your parents traveling abroad?" a Prefect asked me once.

"Yes," I said, obscurely ashamed of never receiving a letter.

Another horror was Mrs. Robley-Smith, the headmistress. She was the Red Queen, with a bosom like a bolster and stiff grey hair and a step that made the floorboards shake. Her behaviour was so bizarre that at first I thought she must be mad till I overheard two sixth form girls talking about her.

"The old girl got such bad hiccups in Geography today that Angela had to go and get her a glass of water," said one, "but she spilt most of it down her jumper."

"Drunk again," said her friend. They rolled their eyes and laughed.

On one occasion after Mrs. Robley-Smith had kept the entire school waiting half an hour for evening prayers, she lurched onto the platform and shouted: "So sorry to have kept you waiting, girls. I thought I was here and I found that I wasn't!" With which she put her elbow on the lectern, missed, and toppled head-first into the front row of juniors sitting cross-legged on the floor.

My one and only interview with Mrs. Robley-Smith concerned a piece of cheese. I'd been unable to eat it at supper because of its patches of hairy green mould, so I'd smuggled it out of the dining hall and hidden it under my mattress, meaning to throw it away later, but I'd forgotten. Now there it sat on Mrs. Robley-Smith's desk, several weeks older and even greener and hairier. I could smell it from across the room.

"Are you aware that food is *rationed*?" she thundered at me. Her quivering bolster-bosom seemed ready to burst with indignation. She flung herself back in her chair and glared at me. Huge earrings like chandeliers swung and jangled from her horrible droopy ear-lobes.

"Well? Well? Speak up, child! Are you or are you not aware that food is rationed?"

"Yes, Mrs. Robley-Smith."

"Do you know how lucky you are to *have* cheese for supper?"

"Yes, Mrs. Robley-Smith."

"Well then, you will now eat this piece of cheese."

"I can't, Mrs. Robley-Smith."

"You will stand there till you do. *Eat it*!"

My hamster habit came in useful. I packed the cheese into my cheek and spat it into my handkerchief as I soon as I'd shut the door of Mrs. Robley-Smith's study behind me.

The bedtime bell rang. Plodding up the back stairs and along the corridors to my dormitory, the reek of moldy cheese mingling with the horrible school smells of carbolic soap and the boiled ham and cabbage there'd been for supper, I wondered how I was to survive the remaining forty-six days of the term—never mind the endless procession of days and terms after that. I ate some toothpaste to get rid of the rancid taste in my mouth and crept into bed.

In retrospect I realize that perhaps if I'd told my parents what the school—and its head mistress—were like they might have taken me away. After all, it was probably very expensive, and they weren't getting very good value for their money.

But they never phoned or wrote or came to see me, and I didn't dare to say anything in the letters we all had to write home every Sunday because the envelopes had to be left open. For "enclosures"—or so we were told.

The only person who came to see me during that endless term was my sister Iris, now a successful fashion model in London. She turned up unannounced to take me out, her aura of glamour and celebrity causing a sensation which swept through the school like a forest fire, bathing me in a temporary glow of reflected glory.

"I say, Diana old bean, rotten luck that you don't look anything like your sister!"

"Got any photos of your sister I could send to my brother at Eton?"

I didn't want to spoil our short time together by talking about school, but Iris had spent most of her childhood in boarding schools so she probably knew anyhow. At any rate when she found out that no arrangements had been made for me for half term, she came and fetched me and took me up to stay with her in her little flat in Chalk Farm in London.

"You know I'm to be married soon?" she said, "You haven't met Teve yet. I've asked him to meet us for tea at the Savoy."

The Pink Drawing Room was packed and noisy, but when Iris swept in, a vision in black velvet and pearls and the highest heels you ever saw, the chatter died away and everyone turned to stare. I shambled after her in my hideous school uniform and shoes like boats, feeling like one of Cinderella's ugly sisters, but proud, too, of my beautiful sister.

My sister, Iris

Teve was partly Portuguese. His swarthy good looks and broad-shouldered 6'3" height made a perfect foil for Iris's white skin and masses of ash blond hair. When he stood up, dashing in his Captain's uniform with its Parachute Regiment insignia and shiny Sam

Brown leather belt and took her hand and kissed it, an audible sigh went round the room.

During his speech at their wedding reception some months later, Teve noticed me lurking behind a tent pole. I was trying to be invisible in a hideous brown dress with stupid little metal flower buttons down the front chosen, needless to say, by my mother. My hair, which was somewhere between wavy and curly and frizzy, was scraped to one side with a Kirby-grip. My mother, in contrast, was a symphony in lilac, not a hair out of place, her face a tribute to the artful skills of Elizabeth Arden.

I realized that Teve had paused in his speech and was smiling at me. His dark eyes seemed to be pinning me to the tent pole. He raised his champagne glass to me and said, "I'm still not sure if I've married the right sister."

The packed marquee erupted in unkind laughter, but I didn't even hear. I was too busy falling in love for the first time.

One Sunday towards the end of my horrible first term at boarding school I was staring up into the vaulted roof of the church when it tilted and swayed and began to revolve. There was a rushing sound in my ears and the next thing I knew I was waking up on the grass among the mossy tombstones in the graveyard. Several people were bending over me saying things like, "She must have fainted," and, "Open your eyes, Daphne dear" and, "I think her name's Diana."

The school doctor examined me and weighed me asked me a few questions and I was put to bed in the Sick Room with nothing to read and nine empty beds for company.

"You're going to have to stay here till you eat something you know, dear," Matron said, not unkindly, as she removed a tray of boiled mutton floating in beads of grease and tapioca pudding sliding across the plate like frog-spawn.

I lost count of how long they kept me there, but one day I was told to get dressed and come downstairs—and there was the Rolls in the drive! My trunk was being loaded into the back by a man I'd never seen before. He was wearing Herbert's grey uniform.

"Spink's the name, Miss," he said, opening the rear door for me, "I'm the new chauffeur."

Sinking into the familiar soft beige leather interior, not quite certain if I was dreaming, I traced a faint hint of my mother's scent to one of her lace-edged hankies, forgotten in the crack between the seats. I rolled it into a tight ball in my hand and I didn't look back as the Rolls purred down the drive and entered the dripping rhododendron tunnel.

Chapter 13

Jinxed

I was so relieved to be escaping from school that I actually forgot for a moment that I wasn't going home. Home was Edwinstowe. The address I'd been writing my Sunday letters to was West Ridge, Reigate, Surrey.

I wondered why we were stopping when Spink drew up after a couple of hours in front of a colossal, sprawling, timbered and tile-hung facade in the style often referred to as "Stockbroker Tudor." The house was supposed to look old, but who was it fooling? For one thing, 1933 was carved into a massive stone slab over the nail-studded front door.

horrible jinxed West Ridge

"Here we are," said Spink.

"This is it?" I asked incredulously, "this is where we live now?"

"Yes, Miss." said Spink getting out of the car and coming round to open the door for me.

While I was trying to get over the shock, one half of the massive front door swung open and out tripped my mother, smiling and as happy as a lark—though she wouldn't be for long. No sooner did we move to Surrey than Sir William's wife Lena, not being a complete fool, announced she wanted to go and live in South Africa. In matter of months the house with the moat and drawbridge had been sold and she'd dragged Sir William off to Durban, plunging my mother into almost terminal despair.

West Ridge was to prove to be an unlucky house for all of us. Sir William's departure would be the tip of the iceberg that nearly sank our family.

"Welcome home, darling!" cried my mother gaily. You'd think I was returning from a successful school term trailing clouds of glory, my trunk stuffed with silver cups and diplomas, not being sent home in disgrace. Out of sight out of mind. Perhaps she'd forgotten where I'd been in the excitement of moving house and being reunited with Sir William.

"Gracious, how thin you are!" she said, giving me a hug. She only came up to my chin now. "Darling! What on earth is this under your blouse?"

I pulled away. I wasn't about to tell her the thing under my blouse was an old crepe bandage Johnny had used for a rugger injury, now being used to flatten the beginnings of my hateful breasts.

"It looks as if we'll have to get you some brassieres," said my mother. Just like that. Right in front of Spink, who was unloading my school trunk.

"Come along, darling!" She seized my hand and bustled me through the front door like a tug boat organizing the Queen Mary. "Wait till you see your new bedroom! It's called the Boudoir. You're going to *adore* it!"

We entered a vast echoing stone-flagged hall. My mother paused to fiddle with an arrangement of salmon-coloured gladioli on the mantle-piece of the phony baronial fireplace. Some of the ox-roasting space was taken up by one of those horrid electric fires with a little flickering red light that was supposed to make the fake logs look as if they were burning.

As we started up a flight of shallow oak stairs, a heavily-built sulky-looking blonde girl in a tight sweater and a tweed skirt with an unraveling hem came stumping down towards us lugging a vacuum cleaner. Its cord snaked behind her, the plug banging on each step.

"Gudren, where's your overall?" said my mother. "And how many times must I tell you to use the back stairs?"

The girl scowled and sighed and turned back, tripping over the cord, dragging the Hoover like a martyr's cross. "Think yourself lucky you didn't get an Order Mark," I told her silently.

"*Au pair girls.*" mouthed my mother. "Quite hopeless, but apparently all you can get in the South."

"But where are Ivy and Violet?" I asked in alarm.

"So inconsiderate, darling. They said they were too set in their ways to make the move."

It had never occurred to me that they wouldn't be coming with us. I hadn't even said goodbye to them properly.

Gudren and her equally surly friend Anna-Marie from Sweden were the forerunners of a procession of foreign au pair girls who were to pass briefly through our lives. They hid the crockery they smashed wrapped in newspaper in the bottoms of the dustbins and helped themselves to my mother's scent and refused to wear uniform and usually flounced off down the drive after a few weeks or months, their suitcases stuffed with towels and writing paper and my mother's cosmetics and silk cami-knickers.

I suppose my pretentiously named new bedroom was pretty if I'd been in the mood to appreciate it.

Its walls were paneled in silvery gray wood, and from the cushioned seat in the deep casement window I could look across the lane to a wood where I was sometimes to hear the bark of a dog fox at night, or the piercing song of a nightingale. There seemed to be at least eight or ten other bedrooms, all with their own bathrooms with everything in matching pastel colours. My mother said it was called *en suite*. My bathroom was big enough to bath an elephant in. Here I was to spend many dispiriting hours examining my changing body in the peach-tinted mirrors and snipping with nail scissors at the hair beginning to grow, (just like poor Ivy), between my legs.

"What's this for?" I asked my mother. I'd never seen a bidet before.

"Oh, it's useful for washing your feet in," said my mother looking flustered. "Darling, do look at these pretty Dutch tiles! All hand-painted!"

Leaning out of my new bedroom window I could hear the faint sound of traffic on the London to Brighton Road, and the pock-pock of tennis balls.

"You must join the Tennis Club in the summer holidays," said my mother. "You can have your father's old racket, and you'll make lots of nice friends."

"But I don't know how to play tennis," I pointed out.

"Don't be difficult, darling."

"What are *you* doing here?" said my father when we encountered each other in the hall a little later. "Aren't you supposed to be away at school?"

"They sent me home."

"Oh? Why?"

"I don't know."

"Hurrumph. I hope you know I've had to lease a field for your horses. *And* hire a horsebox at great expense to get them down here."

"Thank you, Daddy."

"And another thing. That dog of yours keeps trying to run away."

"I expect she misses me."

A phone began ringing in some distant room. He went off to answer it, muttering about damn fool newspaper reporters.

I found my yellow Labrador Suzy shut up in an outhouse. I thought how nice it would be if fathers were half as pleased to see you as dogs were. Suzy and I set off to look for the horses. A gardener pruning roses in a bed about the size of the Isle of Wight directed me to their field.

"Patsy!" I called, "Beauty!" Their heads went up. They neighed with pleasure and came hurrying towards me. Patsy thrust her nose into my collar, blowing her warm breath down my neck, and Beauty's soft lips fumbling my skin with horse kisses felt as comforting as a hug from an old friend you'd bumped into in a hostile country.

Life was completely different at West Ridge. For one thing there wasn't a nursery wing, just a large room at the top of the back stairs set aside for Thomas. It was called the playroom, and contained most of the familiar old nursery furniture.

Patsy thrust her nose into my collar,
blowing her warm breath down my neck . . .

Thomas was six now. Being the youngest by so many years, he was having an even lonelier childhood than mine had been. I often heard him talking to his imaginary friend, Bill Curly. He had a new Nanny called Edith, who seemed to understand; she always set an extra place for Bill Curly at tea time.

Although I was devoted to Thomas it didn't seem to stop me being mean to him. Time and again I'd ride off on Patsy leaving the forlorn little figure gazing wistfully after me in the drive. Why didn't I teach him to ride Beauty and take him with me? When my mother made me give him his bath on Edith's day off I often scrubbed impatiently at his face with the flannel and got soap in his eyes.

Surviving adolescence was making me horribly selfish.

As the au pair girls balked at carrying trays up to the playroom, we started having most of our meals in the dining room with our parents. Such close proximity was a shock. Like adjusting the lens of a pair of binoculars, they were brought into sharp focus for the first time, and I discovered to my astonishment that they were quite ordinary people with quirks and human weaknesses and failings like everyone else.

For example, I noticed that my father didn't seem

Thomas, me, and my dog, Susy

to realize that my mother wasn't listening to a word he said when he ranted on about the Coal Board when he came home from London in the evenings.

"The damn fools hold board meetings to discuss whether to give the miners' children Snakes & Ladders or Ludo for Christmas while the whole industry is going to the dogs!" he'd fume, stamping up and down the drawing room. There was plenty of room for him to stamp at West Ridge. The drawing room was about the size of a football field.

"Mmm," my mother would say, "so annoying for you, darling," and go on with her tapestry, miles away, thinking her own thoughts. She only became interested when there was some major Coal Board rumpus, (usually instigated by my father). and the newspapers got wind of it and started ringing up. She loved talking to reporters.

Another thing was, I found out that my mother told lies! "This old thing?" she'd say when my father asked her if the dress she was wearing was new, "Darling, you must have seen it a million times!" And I'd been with her when she bought it just the day before. Also, she had a special affected telephone voice I'd never noticed before. And the only books she read were novels by people like Mazo de la Roche and Dornford Yates. My father nagged her endlessly about the mess she made of any newspaper she picked up, and he never tired of correcting her grammar, although she took not the slightest notice.

"This is a very good cheese soufflé, isn't it?" she'd say at dinner. No answer.

"I said this is a very good cheese soufflé, isn't it?" she'd repeat a little louder.

My father would give her one of his looks down the table and inquire: "Are you making a statement, which doesn't require an answer, or asking a question?"

My father was far from perfect himself. I soon discovered that he let off whopping farts when he thought no one was about.

This new world was about as disconcerting as going to the zoo and finding they'd done away with the cages and the bears and tigers were wandering around loose.

Another change was that Auntie Betty came to live with us at West Ridge. She and her carriage were installed in a great raftered and paneled room called the Music Room, with a flock of day and night nurses to take care of her. There was no Lassie the donkey to take her for drives any more, but my father bought her a television set—the first any of us had ever seen. Positioned behind the head of her carriage where she could look at it with her arrangement of mirrors, it opened up a world she had never known and would never see for herself; flickering black and white images of the ballet, cathedrals, tropical fish, comedians, aeroplanes, jugglers, chefs, avalanches. The programmes came on for a few hours every evening and there was just one channel, broadcast live from the BBC's studios in London. Most evenings there were technical breakdowns and *Normal Programming Will Be Resumed As Soon As Possible* flashed on the screen, but Thomas and I didn't care. Totally addicted, we were perfectly happy sitting cross-legged on the floor beside Betty's carriage, watching the same bits of film over and over of windmills turning or wheat fields swaying in the wind till the problem was fixed.

Before I could be packed off to another boarding school, I came home from riding one day with a dragging ache in my tummy. When I went up to change out of my jodhpurs for lunch I found flecks of blood on my school knickers. What was the matter with me? Did I have some terrible disease? Was I going to die? Well at least I wouldn't have to go to any more boarding schools, but who would take care of the animals?

By the end of the week I hadn't died—but I had run out of clean knickers. I'd been riding up onto Box Hill and burying them in shallow graves scraped out with my riding crop in the scrubby undergrowth. Then I lay awake at night worrying in case the school name tapes would give me away. I could just imagine some policeman marching up the drive and presenting my father with the evidence of my crime.

It never occurred to me simply to wash my knickers. I'd never washed anything in my life, and had no idea how to go about it. I thought of confiding in Thomas's nanny Edith, but she was a Christian Scientist. She'd probably say if I put my trust in Jesus I'd be cured. My sister Iris might have known what to do, but she was living miles away in Hampshire by then with her husband Teve and their baby.

In the end, in total desperation, I blurted everything out to my mother all among the delphiniums and lilies and peonies she was arranging in the flower room. I decided it would serve her right if I *was* dying. Maybe she'd wish she'd spent a bit more time with me while she had me.

Her reaction took me completely by surprise. "Darling!" she cried, laying down her secateurs and startling me with an emotional embrace. "My little girl's a woman now!"

I was?

In the car on our way home from Boots the Chemist, my mother said suddenly, "Darling, you do realize you can have a baby now, don't you? You mustn't let boys—touch you."

A baby? Boys? What did they have to do with each other? Or for that matter with the contents of the Boots paper bag on my lap? And did boys include my brother Johnny? He was always touching me. Well, twisting my arms or giving me Chinese burns. Did that count?

"You do—understand—don't you, darling?" asked my mother, her eyes firmly on the road.

"Yes," I said.

And that was the end my sexual education until my wedding night four years later.

It had been too much to hope that I could leave school at fourteen.

The uniform at the next school was bottle green, but because of clothes rationing still being in force I had to wear the uniform from the previous school till I grew out of it. In every school photograph I was the odd girl out in grey and maroon.

The new school was neither better nor worse than the last one. Eventually I learned to put myself into a state of semi-hibernation like a bear in a cave, and in this way I survived the lack of privacy, the vile food, the ringing bells, the requirement to have a "crush" on some older girl or mistress. Naturally I didn't learn a thing.

An older girl with long black plaits and blazing dark eyes seemed to want to be my friend. She kept offering me toffees and staring at me a lot.

"Have you got a crush on Jean?" asked one of the girls in my form, "no one else has."

You had to have a crush on someone, but it was advisable to follow the herd and chose someone popular.

"No." I said, and added tactlessly, "I think crushes are stupid."

"Stupid yourself," she retorted, shielding the poem she was composing to the games mistress with her arm.

One night I woke to find Jean, who was our dormitory monitor, kissing and stroking me. I knew it was Jean because there was a full moon and her un-plaited almond-scented hair was all over my face. She was whispering "hush, hush," and trying to get into my bed.

Luckily having a big brother teaches you how to land a good hard punch.

My inglorious school career ended after less than two years, thanks to my father's friend Whiston Bristow.

I'd been drawing and painting all my life, and normally I hated it when my mother said in front of a room full of people, "Darling, do bring your new painting of the horses down and show everyone!"

Whiston was the exception. I liked showing him what I was doing. He understood, and he said sensible, helpful things. One day he asked my parents if he could take some of my paintings away with him.

The next time he came to stay he said, "May I take Diana up to London with me tomorrow to meet an artist friend of mine?"

"If you want to," said my father, who had more important things on his mind like the imminent collapse of his career.

Whiston's friend had a small neat beard, but was otherwise a disappointment. He was wearing a suit and polished shoes like my father's. I'd expected a real artist to be flamboyant and eccentric and covered in paint and have dirty fingernails and fierce black eyes like Picasso.

He and Whiston stood talking and drinking red wine and turning over my paintings and drawings on a paint-splattered table, leaving me free to explore the studio. The artist was evidently a sculptor as well as a painter, and there was almost too much to look at. I jumped when he came up behind me while I was studying a big canvas propped against a wall. It was a landscape with cloud shadows passing over a hillside and several sheep in the foreground. He said. "Well, young lady, what's your opinion?"

"It's *beautiful*," I said sincerely. Then without thinking I added, "but I do think you need to go in a field sometime and have a look at a few sheep. These aren't very good, are they?"

He roared with laughter and slapped his knees and said: "No, they're not. You're absolutely right. I shall take your advice."

In the car on the way home Whiston began to chuckle.

"What's funny?" I asked.

"Do you know who that was?"

"Well yes, you introduced us. Mr.—Wheeler?"

"Sir Charles Wheeler. 'Not very good sheep'." Another burst of mirth. "Oh my goodness. My dear child, he's the President of the Royal Academy!"

When he'd finished snorting and laughing he said: "He likes your drawings very much. He's offering to have you to work in his studio. It's a great opportunity for you."

When my father heard about this proposal he said, "*Alone*? In a studio with some artist feller? Out of the question."

He probably thought all artists were scoundrels and seducers like my godfather Filson.

But thanks to Whiston—or perhaps to Sir Charles—soon afterwards I was offered a place at the prestigious Central School of Art in London. I couldn't start there till I was seventeen, so it was decided that I would fill in the intervening year at the local art school.

Art classes turned out to be surprisingly boring.

"This drawing is very good, but I can't have you putting these black lines round everything," I was told by the hairy life-drawing teacher who reeked of stale sweat and who, I quickly discovered, couldn't draw to save his life. But black lines were what I was doing at that time. If I couldn't do black lines, then I wasn't going to draw at all. I started going to the cinema in the afternoons with a gentle black boy called George instead.

"Diana! I want you in my study. *At once!*" roared my father up the stairs at West Ridge.

"What is the meaning of this?" He thrust a piece of paper into my hand. It was a bill from the art school with a note typed across the bottom.

I read: *It appears that Miss Young feels we have nothing to teach her. As we have a considerable waiting list, we would be obliged if you will remove your daughter from the school at the end of the current term.*

We didn't know it yet, but West Ridge was gearing up to work its sinister alchemy on us all.

The next bad thing that happened was that the progression of Auntie Betty's disease meant she had to be moved into a nursing home, where she very soon died.

"A blessed release," everyone kept saying, but how did they know that? I was sad. I'd loved Betty. I missed her and her mirrors and the way she always listened properly.

Next, there seemed to be something the matter with my mother. She'd practically stopped eating, and was growing terribly thin and was always complaining about being tired. Thomas's nanny Edith was gradually taking over the running of the household from her.

"Pining for Sir William if you ask me," said Johnny, home for the holidays from his Scottish Public School which, if his hair-raising accounts of brutality and depravation were to be believed, made Oliver Twist's orphanage life sound quite privileged.

But I'm ashamed to say that, selfish and self-obsessed teenager that I'd become, my main concern was: *What is to become of ME?*

I soon found out.

Edith helped me to pack my clothes, and Spink drove me up to London and handed me over like an untidy parcel to a bossy French-speaking woman on Victoria Station.

I was on my way to Finishing School in Switzerland.

Chapter 14

Swiss Miss

Whistles were blowing and the train had begun to move out of the station when the carriage door was wrenched open and a couple of suitcases sailed in and a girl with glossy hair like blackbirds' wings scrambled in after them. She slammed the door and lowered the window and hung out, waving and blowing kisses till the train gathered speed.

The French woman spoke to her and wrote something in a notebook and pointed to the seat beside mine.

The girl flung herself down beside me. "Hello," she said in a lilting Welsh accent, "I'm Anne Llewellyn. What's your name? I say, Switzerland! Isn't this a lark?"

Anne would become the first real friend I'd ever had in my life. We're still friends today.

We had to sit up all night, fidgeting and dozing with our heads on each other's shoulders as the train tore across France. The compartment was packed and managed to be both cold and stuffy. We were woken at the border to have our passports examined by French and Swiss soldiers.

The sun rose at last on picture-postcard vistas of trim toy-town villages, neat vineyards and distant snow-capped mountains on the other side of an immense blue lake.

Our escort herded us off the train in Lausanne. After six years of war and rationing and drabness and shortages, the glories of neutral Switzerland burst upon me with the dazzling impact of the first technicolour film I ever saw. I was stunned by the abundance in the shop windows, the air of prosperity, the menu choices in the restaurant where we

were taken for lunch. I'd have been happy just to wolf down the whole bas-
ketful of crusty, fluffy white bread the waiter put on our table. English
bread was still war-time grey stodge. A man at the next table—gabbling
away in French and not looking what he was doing—stubbed out his cigarette *in a whole week's butter ration.*

It began to snow as we arrived in the mountains. Drifts already banked
the twisty road. The school was housed in a cluster of wooden chalets on a
hillside outside the small alpine village of Les Diablerets. Anne and I were
to share a tiny wooden room with a sloping ceiling and doors opening
onto a balcony with stupendous views of glaciers. Instead of blankets on
the beds there were puffy white goose-down duvets. They kept you warm
as toast at night—so long as you could stop them sliding off onto the floor
every time you turned over.

Our school chalet in Switzerland

Meals and lessons took place in the biggest chalet, and five or six girls
lived with a mistress in each of the others. All the girls were English,
(except for one poor Greek girl with a heavy moustache), but in some mysterious way we were expected to speak French to each other the entire

time. Naturally the hills were alive with the sound of piping English voices.

At supper—usually bread and bowls of lentils swimming in what looked suspiciously like spit—we were required to say how many English words we'd spoken that day. Our replies were solemnly entered in a book.

"Caroline Davenport?"

"*Soixante, Madamoiselle.*"

"Mary Foster-Stevens?"

"*Quatre, Mademoiselle.*"

"*Tres bon*, Mary. Diana Young?"

"Er—*beaucoup, Mademoiselle.*"

There were sketchily attended classes in art appreciation, French and English literature, flower arranging, domestic science (useful things like how to plan menus with your cook). Ballroom dancing and skiing were more popular.

Secretarial training was also offered for those adventurous souls among us who were thinking of actually getting jobs. Pitman's shorthand and I parted company after two lessons.

I can't imagine that anyone learned much, and most of us got rather fat, making up for the awful school food by stuffing ourselves with heavenly cakes oozing whipped cream and chocolate at the village *Patisserie.*

It was against the law in 1948 to send money out of England, (I've no idea how the school fees were paid), so the only way our parents could legally send us pocket money was in the form of little booklets

Ann and I

of International Reply Coupons. Officially intended to be exchanged at the Post Office for stamps, a brisk black market was in full swing, and you could cash them in for Swiss francs at half their face value.

Luckily for us, Anne's parents kept her well supplied.

On Saturday nights, lipsticked and curled and bursting out of our sweet-pea dresses, we were taken under heavy guard to the Grand Hotel to practice our social skills and dance with the boys bussed in from the nearby International School in Leysan.

Here for the first time I was exposed to a new and agonizing form of humiliation. Some nervous youth would approach the table where a group of us were gathered, laughing vivaciously and sipping our *jus d'orange* and pretending the last thing we wanted was to be invited to dance.

The boy would wait till he caught my eye, bow, and say, "*Mademoiselle, voulez-vous danser avec moi?*"

Oh, the thrill of being singled out from the crowd for the first time in my life! But then I stood up—and up—and up. And the boy's face froze and turned crimson as he realized that I was going to tower over him like some Amazon. His friends over at the bar were watching and nudging each other and tittering with mirth.

Eventually I learned not to stand all the way up. I found I could keep my knees bent under the full skirt of my long dress for the duration of an entire Fox-trot or Quickstep. This made for a rather ungainly bum-out shuffle round the dance floor, and probably didn't fool anyone—least of all my partner if he tried to move a little closer—only to encounter knees where no knees should have been.

We soon discovered the *après-ski* Tea Dances at the *Patisserie*. There we could flirt with the local boys and the skiing instructors in their glamorous scarlet uniforms and stuff cream buns all at the same time.

Growing bolder, the girls in our chalet were soon knotting sheets together and lowering ourselves down from the balcony of Anne's and my room after dark. Off we'd fly down the road on our toboggans, the cold freezing the insides of our nostrils, out of control, tumbling into ditches, down to the twinkling lights beckoning from the village below. Here we ordered cinnamon-spiced hot wine in the crowded, smoky, fondue-smelling *Auberge de la Poste*, and danced in our thick, oiled-wool ski socks to the music of a piano-accordion played by the jovial *Patron*.

One evening at the *Auberge* I met Rene. He was a medical student from Lausanne whose parents had a weekend chalet in the village and we'd all been yearning after him on the ski slopes for weeks. He was a beautiful skier for one thing, and for another he was extremely handsome, with curly black hair and white teeth and a dark sun-tan.

"*Voulez-vous danser avec moi, Mademoiselle?*" There was no need to bend my knees dancing with Rene. The remembered smell of his crisply laundered shirts lingered long after he'd returned to Lausanne on Sunday evenings, becoming the scent of what I thought must be love.

I became the envy of my friends, and although our romance was far more innocent than I was about to admit, I reveled in my notoriety. Rene wrote me long letters during the week, and my French dictionary finally came in useful. Every evening we gathered on my bed in our dressing gowns with our cocoa, snorting and giggling as we tried to translate the letters.

Handsome Ronnie

"What's *levres?*"

"Just a sec…Here we are. *Lievres*…Hares. He dreams of kissing your *hares?* That can't be right."

"Give it here....Not '*lievres*' stupid. *Levres*. Lips. He dreams of kissing her *lips*. Oh the *bliss*! It's not *fair*! Oh, Diana, you're so *lucky*!"

Lacking a common language, Rene and I couldn't talk much, but it was thrilling to exchange burning looks across the ballroom of the Grand Hotel at the Saturday night dances, right under the noses of our chaperones. Dancing too often with the same boy was regarded with suspicion, and you were supposed to keep six inches between you and your partner at all times, so when Rene crossed the room and invited me to dance we'd be very decorous till he'd maneuvered us into the middle of the crowded floor. Then he'd press me against his swoon-making shirt and murmur in my ear "*Tu es si belle*," which I understood now, and one evening: "*Ah cherie, que j'ai envie de toi*," which I didn't.

Why should he be envious of me? Back to the dictionary. "*Envie*: Desire. Longing." Goodness!

Then one snowy night we came giggling and scuffling back from a merry evening at the *Auberge de la Poste* to find *Mademoiselle* Clara, one of the two headmistresses, huddled in her fur coat on the chalet doorstep. Her face was white with fury and perhaps a touch of frostbite. It was two o'clock in the morning and we knew we were in deep trouble. The previous year there'd been a frightful scandal when an American heiress had actually eloped with a skiing instructor. The school couldn't afford too much of that sort of thing.

It seemed a bit unfair that I was the only one of the five of us to be expelled, but perhaps they'd found out about Rene and his *envie*. I suppose to make an example of me and prevent me contaminating the other girls with my wicked ways, Anne was moved out of our room and I was kept in solitary confinement, my meals sent up on trays, till travel arrangements could be made to send me home. After a few days I was escorted to Lausanne and left on the station platform to wait several hours for the night train to Paris and London.

Luckily I had Rene's telephone number. He collected me in his rattle-trap Deux Chevaux and took me dancing in a smoky cellar with his medical student friends and I nearly missed my train.

By one of those strange quirks of fate, I was to return to Les Diablerets some twelve years later to move into the chalet my Swiss husband had caused to be built just across the road from my old school. He had decided he wanted our children to grow up "speaking better French than their mother," (not difficult), and having seen what I termed the Palace Hotel brats in St Moritz and Davos I had pleaded for a less sophisticated holiday home for our children.

It took a whole year for *Mademoiselle* Clara to bring herself acknowledge my unwelcome presence back, so to speak, on her doorstep. I suppose she felt that anyone wicked enough to be expelled from her establishment deserved to end up in some gutter in Tangiers, not swanning back to the scene of the crime in a socking great maroon Bentley Continental with the back seat full of beautiful blond children.

As the train raced through the night from Lausanne to Paris and London I began to dread facing my father, but in the event I needn't have worried. I got home to find so many bad things happening at West Ridge that my latest fall from grace went almost unnoticed.

My mother was just home from hospital, recovering from major surgery. Her weight-loss and fatigue hadn't, after all, been caused by pining for Sir William. Within days of her return from the London Clinic, Thomas was found unconscious on the bathroom floor in a pool of blood. He was rushed to Great Ormond Street Hospital for Children, where his life was saved by massive blood transfusions. The doctors never did discover the cause of his near-fatal hemorrhage. My father had resigned from the National Coal Board, creating a national uproar but failing, (as he and his supporters had hoped), to bring down the nationalization policy.

And last but by no means least, my Labrador, Suzy, had run away for the last time; she'd been run over and killed by a truck on the London to Brighton Road.

As soon as my mother and Thomas were well enough to travel, my father took them on a Union Castle ship to South Africa to stay with Sir

William, and Johnny returned to Scotland for his last term at public school.

Not knowing what else to do with me, my parents dispatched me down to Hampshire to stay with my sister Iris where, taking up where I'd left off at their wedding, I immediately fell madly in love with my brother-in law.

Chapter 15

Falling in Love with Love?

As the station taxi drew up outside Iris and Teve's thatched cottage the driver said: "Is there a party or sommat?" The narrow lane was jammed with cars parked half in the grassy ditch.

Hearing the taxi, Iris came out to meet me, a baby with wispy black hair lolling on her shoulder. When the driver saw her he stopped exploring his ear with his little finger and jumped out and carried my suitcase to the front door. Iris paid him, and her smile caused him trip over a tricycle as he backed down the garden path.

"Darling! Isn't this lovely?" she cried, "Why haven't you come before? Well, never mind, you're here now. Come in. Mind your head on the door. I've just made tea and someone's brought crumpets. Oops! Another beam. You'll soon learn. Here's the sitting room."

The tiny, low-ceilinged sitting room was rather dark and full of smoke from the log fire crackling in a wide inglenook, and from various pipes and cigarettes. Several men in khaki who'd been sprawled on the sofa and floor and armchairs scrambled to their feet. Iris said, "This is Alex, this is Red. That's Mike over there. Here's Simon and Charlie and that's Andrew. Everyone, this is my sister, Diana. You are all to be nice to her—but not too nice!"

Laughter. They were Teve's fellow officers and all, I soon realized, in love with Iris. Room was made for me by the fire, and Iris's black spaniel Mossy came wagging up and her toddler Sue clutched my skirt with jammy fingers. I was plied with tea and crumpets and welcomed into the warm heart of Iris's world. Teve would be back later from maneuvers on Salisbury Plain.

That evening after the babies were bathed and asleep we had scrambled eggs for supper by the fire. Then we went upstairs and unpacked my suitcase. Iris held up one skirt or dress or blouse after another and dropped them on the floor. "Where did you *get* this stuff?" she demanded, "They look like Mummy's cast-offs!"

"Well, only some."

"And the rest she chose for you?"

"Well, after all, she pays."

Iris sat back on her heels and inspected me. "Listen, there's a party at the Officers' Mess tomorrow night and—wait here, I'll be right back—," she jumped up and left the room. She returned with a dress on a hanger. "You're going to wear this. And, I think, this," she flourished a tiny garment made of white satin and lace and whalebone.

"I'll never get into *that*," I objected.

"Yes you will. Try it on. It's called a Waspy." She hauled me to my feet and made me undress. "Now, take a deep breath while—I—do—up—these—hooks. Now. Look in the mirror."

She turned me round and I gasped—with difficulty because the Waspy made even ordinary breathing difficult. My hated breasts, cradled in satin and rosebuds, were high and round. My waist, confined and molded by whalebone, looked like Vivien Leigh's in *Gone with the Wind*. Well, sort of.

"Now," said Iris. "The dress. Hold up your arms."

I was enveloped in a scented mass of pink and white gingham. Iris pulled the dress down and zipped up the back. "I knew it," she said. "Look at yourself!"

The dress transformed me. It had a flared skirt and a deep frill which left my shoulders and a bit of the tops of my breasts bare. I hitched at the front.

Iris pulled my hands away. "Leave it. That's how it's meant to be."

"But I can't possibly—."

"Can't possibly what? Look beautiful? Darling, you're nearly seventeen! It's time to be beautiful and have fun!"

"But—."

Hearing the taxi, Iris came out to meet me,
a baby with wispy black hair lolling on her shoulder

"No buts. The dress is yours. I can't get into it since the baby anyway. Now, the next thing is—your hair. Let's take this dress off first. Now, come with me—and watch out for odd steps. This cottage is a deathtrap."

"It's not. It's perfect," I said, following her along a twisty passage. Everywhere were low beams and sloping floors and crooked walls and tiny windows nestling under the thatch. Iris had stitched curtains and hung flower-sprigged wallpaper and thrown bright rugs over the sagging sofas and arm chairs. She'd scavenged for antiques and old maps and lamps in local markets and created a small gem on an army shoestring.

We went into the bathroom, which was still steamy and smelling of Johnson's Baby Powder from the babies' baths. The wallpaper here was dark blue with white daisies. Iris sat me down on a stool and dragged a comb through my hair.

"Why on earth hasn't Mummy taken you to a decent hairdresser? I can't believe it. She must have shares in that place she goes to in Dover Street."

She studied my reflection in the mirror, turning my head this way and that. Then she picked up a huge pair of dressmaking shears and started hacking off great chunks of my hair. When she'd finished she washed it and toweled it dry and ruffled it with her fingers and stood back and said, "Tar-rah! You can look now."

She rubbed the steam off the mirror with the towel and my blurry reflection emerged.

I leaned over the washbasin. Was that really me? My flat, wavy, shoulder-length hair was now a sort of big shaggy chrysanthemum, falling round my face in tendrils and leaving the back of my neck bare. For the first time in my life I felt I might be a little bit beautiful.

We heard Teve come in and move about downstairs looking for us.

"Up here!" called Iris. He clomped up the stairs and came into the bathroom, ducking his head, filling the small space. He was wearing battle fatigues.

He stared at me and let out a soft whistle. "Good God," he said. "Who's this?"

"Well? What do you think?" asked Iris proudly.

He put his arm round her, kissed her lips, leaned down and kissed me too. His face was rough with bristles. He smelt of guns and war. He said: "I think I'll be spending tomorrow night fighting off randy subalterns and lecherous old brigadiers."

And he was right!

The Officers' Mess was housed in a primitive sort of a wooden shack, but that night it transformed itself into the Palace of Versailles just for me. My dancing feet barely touched the floor, the harsh overhead lights swung by like chandeliers, the band played the music of the spheres, and the uniformed men who vied with each other to dance with me merged into an aura of male admiration that turned my head far more than the faintly alcoholic fruit cup I was given to drink.

On the way home, Teve said, "Well, How did it feel to be the Belle of the Ball?" In the light of a passing car he smiled at me in the rear-view mirror.

I couldn't tell him the truth. How could I even admit it to myself? How could I confess that the highlight of the evening had been when Teve had put his glass down on the bar and strolled over and tapped the young second lieutenant I was dancing with on the shoulder and waltzed away with me? His hand on my back had pressed me against his glamorous dark blue dress uniform and his eyes had gleamed with amusement as he studied me from under his thick black eyebrows. I'd been afraid he could sense the uproar he was creating under my beautiful pink and white dress.

In the darkness in the back of the car I struggled with guilt and fear and excitement. After everything my sister had done for me, how could I repay her with such treachery? I was ashamed of myself, and ashamed of the fantasies I wove in bed that night.

But not quite ashamed enough to repel Teve's casual flirting. Or to refuse his invitation to join him and Iris in their big bed on Sunday morning for breakfast, all among the toast crumbs and crumpled newspapers and babies and Mossy the dog and Teve's broad, hairy, muscular chest.

And not ashamed enough to resist kisses that even I knew were more than brotherly when he came up behind me when I was washing up in the kitchen, or picking raspberries for supper at the bottom of the garden.

I was out of my depth, and Teve knew it. He enjoyed watching me flounder in the dangerous undertow of awakening sexuality.

Poor Iris. Teve's careless pursuit of her sixteen-year-old sister was nothing new. Even the chubby bespectacled village girl who came to help Iris each morning wasn't safe. If she met him striding out of the cottage in his uniform as she arrived for work she'd come into the kitchen with her glasses steamed up and say breathlessly, "Ooh, that Captain Miller, i'nt he a one? He's got such *smoulderin'* eyes. He makes me come over all funny, he does really."

So overcome was she one morning that when Iris asked her to sweep the garden path, she used the vacuum cleaner. The sound of pebbles flying like bullets and the smell of burning rubber brought Iris dashing out of the cottage too late, unfortunately, to save the Hoover.

Eventually Teve would resign his commission in the army and they would move to South Africa, where Sir William found him a job in Durban. It wasn't long before he ran off with Iris's best friend, leaving her with no money, two children, and a Great Dane called Hamlet.

History had repeated itself. Iris's own father, "the Bounder", had run off and abandoned our mother in much the same way. History would repeat itself again a few years later when Iris met and married an older man and had two more children. Her new husband was the Far Eastern correspondent for the *London Times*, and his job would take them from Durban to Singapore and eventually to glamorous Beirut, still considered at the time to be the Paris of the Middle East.

My parents and Thomas returned from South Africa just in time for the announcement of my father's knighthood. He had first been offered a peerage which he'd declined, being a life-long critic of hereditary titles.

"Frightfully useful for getting good tables in restaurants," pointed out Johnny, who wouldn't at all have minded being the next Lord Young of Bolsover.

"You deserve it, darling," said my mother, totally thrilled. "It's the nation's way of showing their gratitude."

"Rubbish," said my father. "That bloody bunch of politicians in Whitehall just want to shut me up, that's all."

But in the end, and mainly to please my mother, he accepted the knighthood with a not very good grace.

The investiture ceremony in the White Drawing Room at Buckingham Palace was a bitter disappointment to my mother.

"Such *common* people," she complained to Sir William, over from Durban on one of his frequent visits.

The Imperial Society of Knights Bachelor

Know all men by these Presents that His Majesty's Secretary of State for the Home Department having notified unto this Society that on the First day of March. One thousand nine hundred and forty-nine. His Majesty was pleased to confer the Dignity of Knighthood upon

THOMAS ERIC BOSWELL-YOUNG Esq
M.Inst.M.E. A.M.I.C.E.

In consequence and pursuance thereof the said

SIR ERIC YOUNG

has been admitted to be a Member of the Imperial Society of Knights Bachelor and is duly entered in the Society's Roll. In testimony whereof the Seal of the said Society is affixed to this Certificate the same being duly attested by us.

Knight Principal

Registrar

My father's Knighthood

The last straw had come as the King was touching my kneeling father on the shoulders with the ceremonial sword and intoning the ancient command, "Arise, Sir Knight!" and an equerry had to slip discretely between the rows of gilded chairs and ask a woman sitting behind my mother in the audience to stop eating an orange out of a rustling Sainsbury's brown paper bag.

Sir William thought it was hilarious when she recounted this story. "What can you expect, darling?" he said. "With all these jockeys and actors and every Tom Dick and Harry on the Honours List. At this rate there'll soon be more knights than days."

My mother was not amused. She was determined to wring every last bit of prestige out of her new title, and had at once set about stitching an elaborate tapestry fire screen for the drawing room featuring our new coat of arms.

She also embarked on a losing battle with the au pair girls, trying to make them remember to say, "Yes, m'Lady" and, "No, m'Lady" and to refer to her as "Lady Young."

When answering the telephone they were supposed to say, "I'll see if her Ladyship is available," or, "Her Ladyship is not at home," but this seemed to be completely beyond any of them. I once heard a newly arrived Danish girl snatch up the phone and shout crossly into the receiver at some bewildered caller, "The boat, she is out!"

Chapter 16

Who's Afraid of the Big Bad Wolf?

Every weekend now there were blasé young men in tweed jackets and cavalry-twill trousers and suede desert boots sprawled about in the drawing room at West Ridge, drinking beer out of silver tankards and playing records at full volume. Johnny was at the Royal Military Academy at Sandhurst, and the young men were his fellow officer cadets.

"Turn that infernal noise down!" my father would roar from his study as the music thumped down the hall.

Naturally I found them all wildly glamorous, and was ready to fall in love quite indiscriminately with any or all of them. Unfortunately, taking their lead from Johnny, they either ignored me completely or treated me with infuriating condescension.

The truth was that Johnny knew what he and his friends got up to when they all went chasing up to London in the evenings and there was no way he was letting any of them near his little sister.

"I'm not a *child*, you know," I complained to him one day. "I'm *seventeen*, you know."

"Poor old Bones."

"And I wish you'd stop calling me Bones."

"Tell you what," Johnny said as if suddenly taking pity on me, "you can come to the Orchid Room next Saturday if you like." This happened on a Sunday evening. I was lying on his bed watching him pack to go back to Sandhurst.

I bounced up. "The Orchid Room? Next Saturday? I can? Honestly?" The Orchid Room was a *night club*!

"I said so, didn't I?"

I might have known my brother would have an ulterior motive. I followed him out to the drive, and as he slung his bag into the back of his little black M.G. he said casually, "Oh, by the way, why don't you invite that friend of yours—," he pretended to rack his brains for her name, "—Shirley Pierce—on Saturday? Think she'd come?"

She'd come if I had to drag her there in chains with a sack over her head. Actually I was pretty sure she'd come. She probably lived in night clubs.

Shirley was a new friend. She was only a year or two older than me, but light years ahead in sophistication. She even wore *false eyelashes*. My mother thought she was highly "unsuitable," which naturally added to her appeal. Johnny had met her briefly when she came down from London for the night recently.

After she'd gone, my mother had looked up from her tapestry and said, "Darling, I'm afraid your new friend Shirley's underclothes leave a *great* deal to be desired."

I guessed that whichever of the au pair girls had unpacked Shirley's suitcase for her had been cross-examined and reported lashings of black lace and red satin. (Rather than the sensible white cotton my mother considered suitable for girls of our age.) Utterly desirable, in other words.

"Where does—ah—Shirley—live?" enquired my father from behind The Times.

"Streatham," I said.

"*Streatham?*" cried my mother, nearly stabbing herself with her tapestry needle, "darling, *nobody* lives in *Streatham!*"

If snobbishness could turn round and bite you in the leg, my mother would have been well and truly mauled a few years later when, by sheer coincidence, Johnny and Shirley became neighbours in identical palatial Nash terrace houses overlooking Regent's Park.

By then Johnny was married and at the height of his success in the world of shipping and aviation and package holidays, dubbed by the media—who loved his flamboyant ways—"Bow tie Bertie." And Shirley had become Lady Conran, wife of the famed Sir Terence, who was busy transforming frumpy middle-class English houses with Habitat's stylish furniture and terra-cotta pots and baskets. Shirley was a success in her own right, both as a journalist and the author of several best-selling books including how to be a *Superwoman*.

And I bet she was still wearing racy underwear too.

I phoned Shirley as soon as Johnny's M.G. had disappeared down the drive and invited her to the Orchid Room on the following Saturday. She said she'd love to come, and would meet us there.

The London I saw with Johnny on our way to Leicester Square that night wasn't anything like the London I'd seen on the rare occasions we'd been taken up from Edwinstowe when we were children.

In those days we traveled from Nottingham by train in a reserved compartment, and we always stayed at the Savoy. Sabba, the famous Head Waiter in the Savoy Grill Room, was my friend. He knew I hated the complicated Savoy food. "I've got a nice rice pudding for you," he'd whisper out of the side of his mouth as he dealt out the stiff white menus. My parents and Johnny always ordered disgusting things like Quail's Eggs in Aspic and Sole Meuniere and Jugged Hare and I subsisted on bread rolls and kind Sabba's rice pudding.

My other favourite Savoy person was the Concierge. As big as our blacksmith, he wore a splendid dark green gold-frogged uniform, and was in command of an army of grey-uniformed porters and bell-boys. What I admired most about him was the way he could conjure up a taxi with a blast on his small silver whistle and one imperiously raised white-gloved finger. I felt like Princess Margaret Rose when he bowed me into my fold-up seat, and away we'd go, driving on the only bit of road in England where you have to stay on the right-hand side.

Taxis always smelt horribly of wet umbrellas and stale scent and cigars and cigarettes and air that had been breathed by about a million people, but it was worth it; rattling off to Harrods or Madame Tussauds or a the-atre matinee, or on some giddy adventure planned by Sir William. Once he took us boating on the Thames at Bray, and we all nearly ended up in

the river when a swan we'd been feeding with left-over picnic scraps tried
to join us in the punt.

"Where are we?" I asked Johnny on our way to the Orchid Room. We
could easily have been in some foreign country.

"Soho," said Johnny.

It was a warm evening and the M.G.'s canvas roof was folded down.
Exotic scents of garlic, curry, herbs, hot olive oil wafted from restaurant
kitchens and mingled with the pungent smells of pigeons and electricity
and petrol and age-old grime. Multicolored lights and signs glimmered
and flashed. Car horns honked. Laughter and shouting spilled from
upstairs windows. Snatches of jazz, blues, Glen Miller escaped up crum-
bling basement steps whose iron railings had been taken away during the
war to be made into bombs and still hadn't been replaced.

Women wearing thick make-up and tight clothes and very high heels
stood under lamps on street corners, chatting to each other and tossing
their hair. As we edged along in the traffic, from time to time one of them
would wave and call out to Johnny as if she knew him.

"Who is she?" I'd ask.

"Oh, just some prostitute," said my world-weary 20 year-old brother.

"What's that?"

"You know. A tart."

"A tart?"

A sigh. "For goodness sake, don't you know *anything*? They sleep with
people. For money."

"Oh." Why on earth would anyone pay someone just to *sleep*? I put that
puzzle away for later.

Johnny parked the car in a bomb site full of rubble and weeds. The
front of the bombed house was missing, making it like looking into a dolls'
house; there were bits of a staircase, flowered wallpaper, a dangling light
bulb, a bath tub with one claw foot hanging over the edge of an abyss. I
hoped the people had been in an air-raid shelter when the bomb blew their
house apart.

"Now look here," Johnny said as we got out of the car, "You can do what you like tonight, but stay away from Michael Wolfe-Murray."

Just stepping into the purple-draped, dimly lit foyer of the Orchid Room and breathing the perfumed air, I imagined I could feel delicious waves of sin and vice swirling round me. Nanny would have had a fit if she could see me.

I stared at the people milling about, greeting and kissing each other and handing their coats to a pretty blonde girl behind a counter. Shouldn't someone tell her she was about to come right out of the top of her dress? And who were all these people anyway? Where did they come from? You couldn't imagine any of them taking the dog for a walk or worrying about what to be when they grew up.

I caught sight of myself in a mirror and wished I hadn't. I looked like a giant child in my beastly pale blue organdie evening dress.

"What can Iris be thinking of?" my mother had said when I'd unpacked the beautiful low-cut pink and white dress my sister had given me. Seeing the label in the neck she added, "Mr. Dior ought to be ashamed of himself." I never saw the dress again.

Shirley and her eyelashes arrived. She threw off her wrap to reveal a few artfully arranged scraps of black silk clinging to her perfect size zero body. Johnny must have been the envy of every man in the place as he took her arm and led her through a purple curtain into the club. I trailed after them like a pale blue giraffe. On a podium above the packed dance floor a crooner stood in a spotlight in front of the band. "*Funny but when you're near me, I'm in the mood for love,*" she sang in a husky voice. The powdery flesh rising from her black velvet dress swelled and glowed like ripe apricots. There seemed to be a great deal of bare skin about in night clubs. The smoke from about a million cigarettes made my eyes begin to sting and water. Johnny led us through the semi-darkness to a table crowded with his fellow officer cadets and their girl friends. Shirley and I were introduced, but it was impossible to hear anyone's' names above the din.

All except one: Angels announced it with silver trumpets.

Michael Wolfe-Murray. I took one look at him and ignoring, (or possibly ignited by), Johnny's earlier warning, fell instantly in love.

Later in the evening Michael caught me gazing at him and mouthed "Dance?" and inclined his handsome head towards the dance floor. My overheated senses swarmed across the table to him like paper-clips to a magnet. I could hardly get up from my chair.

"Are the stars out tonight? I don't know if it's morning or night, 'Cos I only have eyes for youoo...."

"So," said Michael, taking me in his arms and pressing my eager body against his powerful muscular one, "where has John been hiding you?" He was even handsomer close to, with a lot of silky brown hair falling across his forehead and the thick neck and broad, heavy shoulders of a rugger player. He was much, much taller than me.

"I've been staying with my sister in the country. Before that I was at Finishing School in Switzerland."

He held me at arm's length, inspecting me. "I'd say they did a good job."

Was he teasing me? He had to be teasing me.

He took my hands and put them on his chest. Then he put both his arms round me, fitting me against him even closer. He bent his head and rested his cheek against my chrysanthemum hair. I thought I might drown in the musky, spicy smell of him.

The floor was so packed there was no room to actually dance. We just stood there swaying among all the other swaying couples. I was violently conscious of every inch of my body where it was touching his. Under my skin everything was quivering like Beauty when we went fox-hunting.

"The moon may be high, but I can't see a thing in the sky, 'cos I only have eyes for you—.

What was this hard thing beginning to press against my stomach?

Should I ignore it?

Did Michael know it was there?

Was it—his?

He took his cheek away and looked down at me. His lion-coloured eyes gleamed. *It was—his!* And he knew that I knew it was his. Watching me intently, he relaxed his arms a little, giving me the opportunity to draw back.

I didn't draw back. I'd have fallen down in a heap of pale blue organdie on the dance floor if he'd let go of me altogether. He drew me close again. Now there were the three of us, Michael, me, and *it* swaying to the music. Apparently we were to pretend it wasn't there. Which was about the same as sitting on a beach pretending the giant thing racing towards you over the horizon wasn't a tsunami.

The music stopped and people drifted back to their tables. I thought our dance was over, but Michael kept his arms round me.

"Wait," he murmured. His warm breath on my neck was giving me goose-bumps down my arms. After a few minutes the music started again and the three of us resumed our swaying. "*The very thought of you, and I forget to do, the little ordinary things that everyone ought to do—.*

It was crowded in Johnny's two-seater car till we'd dropped Shirley off in Streatham. He was in high spirits, delighted with the sensation she'd caused among his friends. On the way home he shouted above the warm wind tearing at our hair, "Well, Bones, what did you think of your first nightclub? Did you have fun?"

Fun? What a hopelessly inadequate little word.

When we stopped at a traffic light I asked, "Who was that girl with the piled-up red hair at our table?"

"I dunno," said Johnny. "Annabel something. She's Michael Wolf-Murray's girl friend."

The lights changed and the car surged forward—but not before the little green devil of jealousy had landed on my shoulder and dug in its claws.

I don't know what became of Annabel-something, but much to Johnny's disapproval Michael began telephoning and taking me out. Sometimes we went to the cinema in London, where he put his arm along the back of my seat and breathed in my ear till afterwards I couldn't have told you what the film was even *about*. Once or twice he took me out to dinner, and we had some more thrilling, anxious-making close encounters on dance floors.

Goodness knows the pendulum has swung to the other extreme today, but trust me, in 1949 even the most basic information about sex was incredibly hard to come by. Like money and religion, it was something one didn't talk about.

The letters on the back pages of the women's magazines I scanned in WH Smith's were no help: "Dear Puzzled of Purley, please send me a stamped self-addressed envelope so that I can answer your intimate question privately." The post at our house was brought to my father at the breakfast table. I could just see him accidentally opening a letter intended for "Dear Retarded of Reigate" all among the kippers and the Cooper's marmalade. Novels were no better. Rows of maddening dots "......." took the place of the graphic details Jackie Collins would be dishing out a few decades later. And as for the cinema—the very idea of suave Cary Grant and Doris Day with her perfect hair naked and heaving about among the sheets the way everyone does these days would have been unthinkable.

Having no one to ask, I remained completely in the dark about a topic which was beginning to occupy the greater part of my waking thoughts.

Michael telephoned and said he was going to Paris to play in a rugger match. "Like to come?" he asked.

Please God, let me go to Paris and I'll never bother You again.

One of my daughters told me recently that she believes in the power of "visualization," and maybe she's on to something. I certainly visualized miraculously overcoming a million obstacles, (not the least of which was my father in full battle regalia), and finding myself in Michael's arms beside the Seine with an accordion playing *La Vie en Rose* somewhere nearby.

But as the weekend drew near I began to abandon hope. I didn't know a soul in Paris, I'd never be allowed to go alone, and in any case I had no money. Then the miracle I'd been visualizing and praying for actually happened.

An American friend of my mother's dropped in for tea and said quite casually over cucumber sandwiches in the drawing room, "By the way, Harry and I are off to Paris for the weekend and we thought it would be fun to take Diana along. May we?"

May they? Oh God, I'm going to be such a good person from now on You won't even know me.

We arrived in Paris too late for me to go to the rugger match, but afterwards I stood among the crowds and watched Michael and his fellow soldiers march down the Champs Elysees, pipes skirling, kilts swinging, in the full glory of his Scottish Highland regiment. The British Army had beaten the French Army and Michael was the hero of the hour, having scored the winning try in the last few seconds of the match.

My parents would have had a blue fit if they'd known that their friends' idea of chaperoning me was to say, "Order anything you like from Room Service, honey," before breezing off to a dinner party, leaving me alone with Michael in their opulent suite at the Georges V hotel.

I'll never know if my virginity was protected that evening by my innocence, or by Michael's moral scruples, or by some prior threat of retribution from Johnny. Maybe a bit of all three.

But when Michael drew me down among the gold brocade cushions on the sofa after supper and took my face in his hands and kissed my lips, I'm almost certain that an accordion began to play *La Vie en Rose* in the street below.

Chapter 17

On the Shelf

There were no more officer cadets sprawled in the drawing room drinking beer and enraging my father by playing Peggy Lee singing *Teach me Tiger* at full volume.

Johnny and Michael Wolfe-Murray and their friends had passed out of Sandhurst in a blaze of glory with brass bands playing and flags flying and

Johnny, 2nd Lieutenant
In the Green Howards

royal personages saluting and gone off to join their regiments abroad. Michael was in Germany, where he soon stopped answering my witty casually dashed-off letters which had taken so many hours and pen-chewing to compose. Johnny had joined our father's infantry regiment in Malaya, where the British Army was engaged in bloody jungle warfare against the communist guerrillas.

To my dismay, about this time my mother began to worry about my social life—or lack of it. Her solution was to make me start going to dances held by her friends in their houses for their teenage children. Those dances were every bit as bad in their way as the parties I'd had to go to at the Duke of Portland's stately pile when I was little.

The host parents circled the dance floor all evening like a couple of anxious sheepdogs, clapping their hands and jollying us along with cries of, "Now everyone! Time for an "Excuse Me" dance!"

We also had to be statues, hold oranges between our foreheads, or pass broomsticks around till the music stopped.

The same moth-eaten trio played the same selections from '*Annie Get Your Gun*' and '*Oklahoma*' at all the dances: *The girl that I marry will have to beee as soft and as sweet as a nursereee—*.

The dance I dreaded most of all was the Paul Jones. For this everyone had to hold hands, the girls forming an inner circle, the boys facing them in an outer circle, and round you went in opposite directions till the music stopped. Then you were supposed to dance with the boy facing you. Since there were always a few more girls than boys, you were liable to find yourself stranded in the middle of the floor being smirked at over their partners' shoulders by the luckier girls. If you tried to sneak off to sit on the coats on a spare bed for a bit, one of the sheepdogs was bound to come snapping at your heels and herd you back.

There was fruit-cup like red ink with bits of orange floating in it to drink, and a Buffet Supper laid out in the dining room; sausage rolls, things on toothpicks or in aspic, fish paste sandwiches cut in triangles, trifle and meringues and hectic-coloured jellies in little fluted paper cups.

The relief when eleven o'clock came and our exhausted hostess called brightly, "Diana! The car is here for you!" and I could sink into the back of the Rolls and go home.

In the morning it would be, "Did you have a lovely time, darling?"
"It was all right."
"Did you meet anyone nice?" Meaning a boy, of course.
"No."

A sigh. "Oh, the dances when I was a girl! I don't know what's the matter with you young people these days."

One of the things the matter with me was that I seemed to have acquired a taste for Older Men. Men in Uniform. Schoolboys with hot hands wearing their fathers' dinner jackets didn't interest me in the least.

"When is that girl going to get a job?" my father began asking. When indeed? And doing what?

Perhaps I could become a dress designer and dash off sketches of ball gowns and wedding dresses, or revolutionize the frumpy appearance of the ladies of the Royal Family.

A few months wrestling with the mathematics involved in learning to cut out paper dress patterns in the damp neon-lit basement of the Katinka School of Fashion Design in Kensington soon cured me of that idea. The BBC seemed another possibility. I would write sensitive television plays about misunderstood teenagers. The only trouble was, the BBC wouldn't even give you an interview unless you could do shorthand and typing.

About this time horrible jinxed West Ridge was put up for sale. Prior to my parents' eventual departure to live in South Africa, we were apparently to move to a house in rural Buckinghamshire.

One day as I was returning from riding, a big black car swept by and a man turned round and looked at me out of the rear window. When I arrived home and came back from putting Patsy in her stable, I saw that the same big black car was parked in the drive.

I found my mother showing an elderly couple of potential purchasers round the house. They were accompanied by the man I'd just seen in the back of the car. He was wearing *blue jeans*!

Blue jeans were the very latest thing from America, but you couldn't buy them yet in England so I'd persuaded a friend who worked on the Queen Mary to bring me back a pair. The first time I swaggered into the drawing room wearing them, a cocktail party was in progress. My father scowled at me from across the room and said in a loud voice, "Take no notice of her. She's come to see to the drains."

I hoped he would stay in his study today. I could just see him directing this good-looking man and his jeans to the tradesman's entrance.

My mother introduced me. The couple was Swiss, and both had heavy accents. The man with them had a faint American accent and was about a foot taller than either of them, but he was their son and his name was Walter.

"Diana!" my father shouted from his study, "That damned horse of yours is out again! She's trampling the asparagus bed!"

I raced out to catch Patsy and Walter came to help me, little knowing what a narrow escape he'd had.

"If you get me a screwdriver I'll fix this bolt on her door," he offered when we'd got Patsy back into her stable.

While he was tightening the loose screws I had the chance to have a good look at him. He had fair wavy hair and blue eyes. Dark and dangerous Teve or Clark Gable as Rhett Butler were more my type, but Walter was undeniably handsome. I also noticed that he had particularly beautiful hands; big and knuckly with spatulate fingers. There was a heavy gold ring on the third finger of his left hand.

Walter

"There," he said, testing the bolt, "that should do it."

"Are you married?" It just slipped out. What an idiot! I could feel a blush starting up my neck.

Walter laughed. "Married? Me? Good heavens no!"

While I gave Patsy some hay, he lounged in the stable doorway and told me a bit about the three years he'd just spent in America. He and a friend had driven 3,000 miles from New York to San Francisco. He'd nearly been mauled by a bear in Yellowstone Park, been held up at gun-point in Nevada, and taught skiing in Sun Valley. The Korean War was going on and he'd been conscripted into the American Army, where he'd learned to play polo and had driven a tank down 5th Avenue in New York in a parade. He spoke French and German and Italian.

I was deeply impressed. I had no idea that such people or such adventures existed in real life. When he asked me about myself I muttered something pathetic about finishing school in Switzerland.

"*Alors, tu parles francaise?*" said Walter.

"*Non.* Not really."

He smiled. He had nice teeth. One was slightly crooked. "Well you're pretty young. You've plenty of time to learn."

"I'm not *that* young!" I said crossly. "How old are you?"

"I'm twenty-six."

An older man!

I was about to have my eighteenth birthday and there was to be a party at a local hotel. The thought of the boys—the *children*—my mother was bound to have invited, (the same ones who trod on my feet at her friends' horrible teenage dances), compared to this worldly, sophisticated, much-traveled man was too boring to think about. We heard a car horn in the drive.

"I guess my parents are ready to leave," said Walter. *I guess.* What heaven—just like in an American film.

We strolled back to the house. The sun was going down, and our shadows went before us across the lawn. The top of my head came up to his ear. Obviously I'd never see him again. Who in their right mind would want to buy beastly West Ridge?

"What a handsome young man," said my mother after they'd gone, "didn't you think so, darling?"

"I didn't really notice."

My mother laughed. "Ah-ha! Methinks the lady doth protest too much!"

Grrr.

Later, in my bathroom mirror, I tried to see myself through Walter's eyes. It wasn't encouraging. Too tall. Hateful breasts. Not an interesting hollow or a hint of a cheekbone in my stupid baby-face. Half grown out chrysanthemum haircut going into kinks because it had started to rain while we were catching Patsy.

Look on the bright side, I told myself. After all it was *me* Michael invited to Paris, not Annabel-something. And hadn't Rene picked me out of the crowd in Switzerland? We'd even written to each other for a while after I was sent home, but I got sick of struggling with irregular French verbs, and then I met Michael.

When Rene wrote saying he wanted to come to England to see me, I'd written back telling him I was going away—possibly for ever—to Peru. Why on earth did I pick *Peru*? I didn't even know where it was.

The night Michael had kissed me in the Paris I'd been sure it was true love at last. Wrong, obviously, or he wouldn't have stopped answering my letters.

I'd better face it, I thought glumly, no one was ever going to love me or want to marry me. I was going to end up an old maid like Thomas's nanny Edith, and probably become a Christian Scientist.

A few days after my birthday it was raining as usual and my mother said, "Oh do stop mooning about the house, darling. If you've got nothing better to do, you could take Thomas to the cinema this afternoon. He's been begging to go."

"It's a stupid film. Probably the most stupid film ever made."

"Well he wants to see it so badly." She couldn't resist adding a little lecture. "Good things happen to people who do unselfish things in this life."

Oh sure. But I took Thomas to his film, which at least made him happy. And for once my mother proved to be right.

"Walter's mother rang up while you were out," she said. "So polite and charming. I expect it's a Swiss custom."

"What is? What did she want?"

"She wanted to know if it would be all right if Walter invited you to a party on New Year's Eve."

Would it be all right?

Walter arrived to collect me for the party in a beautiful cream-coloured, drop-head Jaguar with red leather seats and he definitely wasn't wearing his father's dinner jacket.

The party was at a country club on the other side of London and on the way we stopped at his apartment because he'd forgotten the tickets.

His apartment was above a restaurant in Curzon Street called the Mirabelle. I'd never seen anything like it except in Hollywood films. Everything was white; white carpet, white furniture, white flowers. Even the little *radio* was white. He went into the tiny white kitchen and took a bottle out of the white fridge and poured us each a glass of white wine.

I didn't like the taste of it very much, preferring sweet things like Asti Spumanti, but I drank a bit to be polite. Then we went to the party.

When the girl with the band started crooning, *"I'm in the mood for love, simply because you're near me...."* Walter stood up and said, "Shall we dance?" He held me very formally the way they did in *Come Dancing* on television: elbows out. I tried not to think about practically falling down with excitement when I was being crushed against Michael Wolfe-Murray's manly chest (and other parts) on various dance floors.

At midnight the balloons and streamers fell around us and people screamed and kissed and hugged and blew whistles and hooters and Walter kissed me on both cheeks the way they do in Europe and said, "Happy New Year!"

Years later, I found out that he told someone in our party that night, "That's the girl I'm going to marry."

Chapter 18

Love's Young Dream?

Believe me, it's a really bad idea to start going out with someone if his parents are trying to buy your parents' house.

Walter's father was Swiss-German and he might have got on a bit better with my father if his strutting walk and mustache weren't so dangerously like Hitler's. His mother was Swiss-Italian. She was fat and jolly and owned a vast array of mink and sable coats and hats and jackets. The ropes of pearls as big as marbles which cascaded down her front were, my mother admitted, almost certainly real. Her poor feet bulged dreadfully over the sides of her fashionable Charles Jordan shoes, and she obviously didn't believe in deodorant, and must have lived on garlic.

My father's face was a study each time they came back to look at the house again and she heaved herself out of the car and came rocking across the drive to shake his hand. Even lavish applications of *Joy* failed to entirely mask the whiffs of armpit and garlic.

My mother didn't care about his parents—she was entranced with Walter. She loved his rather formal European manners and beautifully laundered shirts and the way he always brought her flowers when he came to take me out. She obviously saw in him a possible solution to the question of what was to become of me. A knotty problem which was probably delaying her departure for South Africa and Sir William.

In spite of *1933* carved over the front door, Walter's father seemed to be under the extraordinary impression that fake and phony West Ridge was a genuine Elizabethan manor house. I discovered later that buying it was supposed to advance his plan to join what he quaintly called "the landed gentry."

165

When I introduced him to Patsy and Beauty he said, "The landed gentry have many horses. I must remember to buy a horse."

Poor horse, I thought, seeing the way Patsy shied away from the hand he raised to pat her. Horses and dogs are often much better judges of character than people are.

A price was finally agreed on for the house, but then the haggling over the fixtures and fittings began. For a few tense days the entire sale hung in the balance over the hideous fake-log electric fire in the hall. Incredibly, my mother was reluctant to part with the horrible thing and Walter's mother was determined to have it. I found out later that she had a passion for bargaining. She treated Harrods like an Arab souk. "*Forty-six pounds?*" she'd exclaim in disbelief over some silk scarf, "I'll give you thirty for it. Cash." You should have seen the assistants' faces.

A dispirited layer of snow lay on the ground as January dragged on and the house sale negotiations with it. To escape the embattled atmosphere at West Ridge, Walter and I went down to Knapp Cottage to stay with Iris and Teve for the weekend.

"You seem to have a thing about the Swiss," teased Iris when we were washing up the supper things. I'd told her about Rene.

"You'd hardy know that chap of yours is a foreigner," said Teve, cornering me outside the bathroom for an unbrotherly goodnight kiss.

On Sunday morning I took Walter up a mug of coffee in bed. He'd been put in my old room, and as usual the bed had crept across the sloping floor in the night and wedged itself under the window. His blue pajamas were open at the neck and I was fascinated by the glimpse of pale gold hair on his chest.

"Don't go," he said, and I put his coffee down and perched on the edge of the bed. He drew me to him and started giving me little all-over-my-face kisses. They reminded me of the butterfly kisses I used to give Granny Ting with my eyelashes.

The door opened and Iris stuck her head in. "Oops! Sorry!" she said, then she added cheerfully, "By the way, are you two engaged yet? Because if you're not Teve says we can't have champagne for lunch."

What was she *thinking* of?

But Walter just smiled and said, "Well, that doesn't leave us much option, does it?"

Iris laughed. Then a crash and a series of thumps and wails sent her flying downstairs to separate her children. Walter looked at me.

"Would you like to get married?" he said. "Darling, would you like to be my wife?" It was the first time he'd called me darling.

No more nagging about when was "she" going to get a job. And for once I'd be in my mother's good books—.

Walter was watching me. His eyes matched his pajamas. Why on earth would he want to marry *me*?

"Yes."

Did I just say that?

I must have, because Walter said "Good." He took the heavy gold ring off his finger and put it on mine. "Just till I can get you a proper engagement ring," he said.

"Thank you," I said politely.

And that was that. I wouldn't be an old maid like Edith after all.

The champagne bubbles got up my nose rather at the lunch party Iris had organized and I didn't like the taste much, but it was exciting being the centre of attention.

Iris and Tom would soon be off to live in South Africa. When we left on Sunday night I wondered when I would ever see my sister again.

"Be happy, darling," she said hugging me in the hall while Walter was putting our cases in the Jaguar. She scanned my face. "You're quite sure you really love him, aren't you?"

"Oh yes," I said.

She seemed about to say something else, but then Teve appeared and then it was time to go.

Driving back to Surrey, I kept glancing at Walter's handsome profile in the lights of the oncoming traffic. What was it about one person that just being *near* them could thrill you to the marrow of your bones? Why wasn't it up to you to decide who made you feel like that? I so *wanted* to feel it about Walter.

I twisted his ring on my finger. It was much too big. I'd have to be careful not to lose it.

"You're very quiet," Walter said. He took one hand off the wheel and put it on mine. "Are you happy, darling?"

"The thing is, I'm not sure if I really love you." I hadn't known I was going to say that. It just came out.

Walter was silent for a moment. Then he said, "I think that's because you're very young. You don't know much about love, do you? You'll see, it'll be all right when we're married."

"Oh," I said, wanting to believe him. "Are you sure?"

"I'm sure," he said. "Trust me."

And that was the moment which decided the next twenty years of both our lives.

We stopped at the hotel on the Hog's Back for supper and I telephoned West Ridge. My mother answered.

"Walter has asked me to marry him," I said. I had the oddest feeling this was happening to someone else and I was just reporting it. I picked at a flake of depressing brown paint in the phone booth. The receiver had recently been wiped over with disinfectant.

"Darling!" cried my mother, "How wonderful!" She didn't even ask me what I'd answered. She just *assumed*. "Where are you?"

I told her.

"Good," she said, "I'll have time to cope with your father before you get here."

Cope? Years later I found out that when she broke the news of my engagement to my father, he flew into a rage and roared, "Why can't she marry an Englishman? Not some bloody Kraut!"

"No, no, darling," soothed my mother, "you know perfectly well Walter isn't German. He's Swiss—."

"Swiss? Swiss? What the devil did *they* do in the war? Bunch of bloody shirkers—."

But by the time we arrived and my father took Walter off to his study to interview him about his ability to support me, he'd calmed down and my mother had won.

She was also going to win the competition among her friends to see who could get their daughters married off first. Over the next few months I'd hear her on the phone: "My dear, talk about love's young dream! I can't get any sense out of her—yes, foreign, of course, and quite a bit older, but from a *very* good family—."

If she'd been born a bit later my mother could have had a great career writing soap operas.

During the summer of our engagement, Walter was allowed to take me to the West Country on holiday—on condition that his married sister and her husband came along as chaperones.

Yvonne was pregnant, and we had to keep stopping the car for her to be sick. But the weather was lovely and Cornwall was still a place of few tourists and sweet little fishing villages and deserted coves and beaches. Walter bought me a Cornish silver ring set with moonstones which I liked much better than my engagement ring with its half-inch chunk of diamond.

A popular song kept playing the whole time on the car radio:

If ever a pair of eyes
promised paradise,
deceiving me, grieving me
lea-eaving me blue—
it was you, Jezebel,
it was you.....

Walter hummed along with it and smiled at me in the rear-view mirror, making me extremely nervous, squashed in the back with Yvonne.

Naturally I had no intention of deceiving him or grieving him or leaving him blue, but I wasn't at all sure about being able to promise him much in the way of paradise.

Walter's parents gave us an adorable mews cottage in Chelsea with a blue front door and geraniums in the window boxes as a wedding present. My mother called it The Dolls' House—which was nearer the truth than she knew. If I could have bought plates of plaster food for the kitchen I'm sure I would have.

My parents matched this magnificent gift with five hundred pounds and a bunch of old family silver no one wanted any more—including me. I stuck it in the back of a cupboard where it soon turned navy blue. Some

. . . an adorable mews cottage
in Chelsea

twenty some years later I sold it and used the proceeds to go to Hawaii.

Relations between the two families—already strained during the sale of West Ridge—took a turn for the worse over the discrepancy between the wedding presents.

My future father-in-law's basic hatred and mistrust of the English, who had been snubbing and patronizing him for years the way we usually do bumptious foreigners, came to the fore. He obviously felt he'd been misled by my father's title and our "Tudor" mansion and the au pair girls and the Rolls in the garage. Could it be that he'd made a terrible mistake, and we were neither aristocratic nor wealthy?

If so, an alliance between our two families wasn't going to give him the leg-up into "the landed gentry" he so craved in order to get his own back for all those years of snubs and insults. As for my father, he remained unconvinced that there was any real difference between "Swiss German" and "German."

The gulf between the two families became the Grand Canyon, howling with social discord, when we were invited to dinner at West Ridge a few months after Walter's parents moved in. Even at the best of times it's weird going back to a house you once lived in and seeing what the new owners have done to it—and these were not the best of times.

"Would you like to look round?" my parents were asked when we arrived.

"Whatever for?' said my father, who was looking forward to a whiskey and soda after the traffic driving over from Buckinghamshire.

"We'd love to," said my mother diplomatically.

Walter's parents were obviously fug rats. None of the windows could have been opened since we left, and a miasma of cigarette smoke hung over everything. Our faded Persian rugs had been replaced with acres of peach-coloured fitted carpets that you sank into up to your ankles, and instead of the old silk and brocade curtains, the windows were now shrouded in net. Rooms once furnished with Sheraton and Chippendale and Hepplewhite contained colossal "suites" and matching sets of reproduction furniture, mainly Jacobean in style.

Most of the rooms, though crammed full of furniture, appeared to be closed up and not in use. My father was finally given his whiskey and soda in what used to be his study—now re-named The Den. There was no sign of any servants. Did Walter's poor mother do all the housework and cooking herself? You needed roller skates just to get around the kitchens.

Dinner—whoever had cooked it—was a tense affair.

"Can you tell me where I can hire a flame-gun?" Walter's father asked my father during the main course (heavy on the garlic—an illegal substance in our house).

"A flame-gun? What on earth do you want a flame-gun for?" demanded my father.

It was explained that the gardens, which had recently featured in 'House & Garden' magazine, were to be razed and ploughed up and electric fencing installed to accommodate a horse.

Later, Walter's father would engage an excitable Polish Count to teach him to ride. When Walter and I were staying at West Ridge one weekend after we were married I heard them yelling at each other among the clods of earth in the devastated garden.

"I'm *paying* you to teach me to ride this horse!" screamed my father-in-law.

"My dear sir," responded the Count, "there is not enough money in the world to turn you into a horseman!"

No one said anything for a while in the car on the way home from the disastrous dinner party.

Then my mother said, "Net curtains. No servants. Very *odd,* isn't it?"

"A flame-gun," said my father.

They were quiet for a bit, then my father said, "Funny blighters, foreigners."

It didn't seem to occur to them that they were discussing my future parents-in-law.

But I was busy with my own thoughts in the back of the car. I was wrestling once again with the mysteries of *class.* Walter's father was very wealthy—probably as wealthy as Sir William—but he obviously wasn't a gentleman—not even one of nature's variety. For one thing he held his knife like a pen, which even I could have told him was the kiss of death for anyone aspiring to the "landed gentry." For another he said 'garrige' instead of 'garaaage.' And when he sloshed a bottle of Sandiman's Tawny Port into a square whiskey decanter and passed it the wrong way round the table after "dessert" at dinner I didn't even dare to look at my father.

But if his father wasn't a gentleman, did that mean that Walter wasn't either? And if my parents were so keen on people being gentlemen, surely they'd mind me marrying someone who wasn't?

In bed that night I came to the conclusion that they were so relieved to be getting me married off that they'd decided beggars couldn't be choosers.

On my wedding morning I was given breakfast in bed although I was feeling perfectly well. One of the au pair girls came barging in with the tray and banged it down on the bedside table and wrenched back the curtains. January rain was lashing the trees and streaming down the window.

Ingrid fingered my lace and tulle wedding dress hanging on the back of the wardrobe door. "Tonight it is the night, eh?" she said. I ignored her. She giggled and flounced out, banging the door. She was leaving at the end of the week anyhow.

The toast was burnt and they'd forgotten the marmalade, but I was quite enjoying the luxury of breakfast in bed when the door opened and in came my mother. The last time I'd seen her this early in the morning was when a stray German incendiary bomb fell on the roof at Edwinstowe during the war.

"Good morning, darling. Did you sleep well?" All this concern for my welfare. I felt like a laboratory beagle.

My mother started rustling tissue paper and reorganizing my honeymoon suitcase which was standing on a chair. It had my new initials on the side. How was I ever going to remember I had a new name?

"Really, darling!" said my mother, "Whatever would Walter think?" She removed my teddy-bear from under the slithery satin *negligee* which was replacing my school dressing gown and put him on the bookcase.

"Darling," she said, still rummaging busily and keeping her back to me, "Is there anything you'd like to ask me about? Anything that might be—ah—worrying you?"

I knew what she was getting at: the information I'd hunted for in vain on the back pages of women's magazines and in novels. But my mother and I had never talked about such matters before. It seemed a bit late to start now.

I stirred my tea and said politely: "No thank you."

She stopped messing about with my suitcase, but I could see she didn't feel her duty was quite done yet. "You do—love—Walter, don't you, darling?" she asked.

I wondered what would happen if I hurled my tea cup across the room and yelled at her: "How do I know if I love him? How can I tell? I hardly know him! I don't know anything about men! Or love! Or life!"

Instead I said, "Oh yes."

But I was remembering the time when Walter kissed me goodnight and tried to stick his tongue in my mouth.

"Stop it! I hate that!" I'd said, pushing him away.

"Don't worry," he'd replied, quite unruffled, "You'll like it when we're married."

But would I? *Why* would I?

Anyway I wasn't about to get into a conversation with my mother about men's tongues or their weird interest in your breasts or what went on inside their trousers. She probably wouldn't be much help anyhow. I couldn't imagine my father sticking his tongue in *her* mouth. But after all Walter was Swiss. Although it had never happened with Rene, perhaps it was a Swiss custom—like Eskimos rubbing noses. If Walter tried it again, I'd just have to tell him it wasn't done in England.

My mother was moving towards the door. Thinking I should make her feel her visit hadn't been a complete waste of time, I said, "Actually there is one thing worrying me rather."

She froze, her hand on the doorknob. You'd think I'd impaled her to the door with an arrow between her shoulder-blades.

She took a deep breath and turned to face me. "What's that?"

"I wish I knew how to cook."

My mother laughed gaily. "Oh, I shouldn't worry about that if I were you, darling," she said, "I'm sure you'll soon learn."

How could she be sure? So far as I knew my mother had never set foot in a kitchen in all her married life. Not unless you counted the time at Edwinstowe when a poor little scullery maid had an epileptic fit and lay thrashing about on the kitchen floor, foaming at the mouth with a wooden clothes peg clenched between her teeth, till my mother arrived with Doctor Gray.

"I'll tell Ingrid to run your bath," said my mother. "I'd better go and help your father. His morning suit always makes him cross."

When they'd zipped up my wedding dress and arranged my veil and made sure I was wearing *Something Old, Something New, Something Borrowed, Something Blue,* everyone left for the church and I was alone in the house with my father.

I came downstairs and found him in the dining room, pouring himself a brandy from a decanter on the sideboard.

"You'd better have a small one too," he said. "Steady your nerves."

I wasn't feeling nerv-

Father of the bride

ous. If anything, I was feeling numb. *She moved towards her destiny in a trance.* I rather liked that. I must remember to write it down in my journal. I might grow up to be a famous novelist. Except that my journal was mostly blank pages or sketches of horses.

My father was looking very handsome and distinguished in his detested morning clothes. As he handed me my brandy he took in my own transformed appearance.

"My dear, you look—beautiful," he said, and to my amazement I saw tears well up in his eyes. He put our glasses down and took me in his arms, crushing my dress and veil.

"Be happy, little Queenie," he said gruffly.

It was the sweetest moment I had ever experienced with my father. For the first time I felt that in his remote and unapproachable way perhaps he loved me after all.

Standing in his embrace, inhaling the mingled scent of mothballs and the white carnation in his buttonhole, I wished that time would stand still. Instead it reeled back and I was a child again, and my father was sitting by my Welsh hospital bed teaching me to play Whist after I'd had my appendix out. I saw his face when I presented him with the gift of an unexploded bomb.... What would he say if I told him I wasn't sure about getting married? Perhaps he'd stop it happening.

"Daddy—"

"Yes?"

But at that moment Spink knocked on the door and it was time to get into the Rolls with its fluttering white ribbons and drive through the rain to the church.

As we turned out of the gates, I looked back at the house. I was leaving my family's home for the last time as the me that I knew. When I came back in future it would be as a married woman, a visitor, and I'd sleep in a spare bedroom with Walter.

And soon my parents would be going off to live in South Africa and there'd be no home to come back to at all any more.

So many losses: Edwinstowe. The forest. The village. Nanny and Bear and Auntie Betty. Ivy and Violet and Cartledge. My dog Suzy. Patsy and Beauty, (given away to a girl who loved them.)....

I swallowed the lump in my throat. The scent of the gardenias Walter had had flown in especially for my bouquet was making me feel rather sick. I glanced at my father through my veil. He was staring straight ahead, looking stern and turning the brim of his top hat round between his fingers.

But his hand when he helped me from the car outside the church was warm and firm. I wished I could have had it to hold sooner in my life.

The church was pretty embarrassing.

The bride's side was packed with a sea of bald heads and floral hats belonging to relatives and my parents' friends. Among them I spotted Anne and the couple of girls I'd grudgingly been allowed to invite.

On the bridegroom's side sat Walter's parents in solitary state—except for Yvonne, who was either pregnant again or hadn't got her figure back, and a stray uncle who dealt in furs at the Hudson's Bay Company. He was probably responsible for the faint stench of rotting animal pelts mingling with the scent of lilies.

My three friends, none of whom were married yet, turned to stare at me with open curiosity as the organist crashed into the opening chords of "Here comes the bride," making me wonder uneasily if I was some sort of a matrimonial guinea-pig.

But then I felt my father urging me forward and I was being led up the aisle, clutching my gardenias and attended by a cousin who was probably about as ready to get married as I was, although she was only twelve. Through the mists of my veil I saw Walter waiting for me at the altar, elegant and debonair in a pearl grey morning suit.

The solemn, binding words of the marriage service began.

When the moment came for the vicar to look out over the congregation and enquire if anyone knew of any just cause or impediment why we should not be joined together in holy matrimony my tummy gave as tiny, treacherous lurch. But no one spoke up.

And then Walter was putting the ring on my finger and vows were exchanged and blessings bestowed and he was turning back my veil and kissing me.

After the registry had been signed, Mendelssohn's Wedding March rolled and vibrated through the church and I was walking beside my husband, (*my husband? my husband!*), back down the aisle past all the hats and flowers and smiling faces. I saw affectionate smiles, phony smiles, moistly sentimental smiles, polite smiles and a few frankly impatient smiles—probably due to a desire to get at the champagne at the reception.

Past all the smiling faces we walked, Walter and I, out into the rain and the confetti and the clamour of bells. Out into the future we were to share together—though not, as things would turn out, till death did us part.

Postscript

September 2005. Sun Valley, Idaho, USA.

My friend Paula and I are sitting in the green shade of the garden parasol with mugs of tea. The humming birds are zooming round their red plastic bird-feeder like tiny Spitfires in the Battle of Britain. Water splashes in the fountain and bumble-bees stagger among the hollyhocks and the dogs lie panting under the nearby willow tree. It is 90 degrees. It hasn't rained since May and the sage-covered hills are bleached with draught. The surrounding mountains tower against the brilliant sky, dramatic and improbable as cut-out stage scenery.

Like me, Paula is in her seventies now. She once danced with the New York City Ballet and still teaches dancing, and, like her beloved cats, is incapable of a graceless movement—though she claims to be riddled with arthritis.

She lights one of her long brown cigarettes. Our doctor has told her to stop smoking. "Young man," Paula told him firmly, "I am *seventy three years old!*"

Leaning forward, she picks up a bundle of stapled papers off the table. She reads aloud, *This Girl's Life*. What's this?"

"My granddaughter Serena's autobiography. She just sent it to me from Maui."

"How old is she now?"

"Thirteen."

We smile at each other, amused and charmed. We're probably both wondering what Serena will be writing about when she's our age.

I say, "It's partly because of Serena that I decided to write this book I'm working on."

"How come?"

"Well, I was watching her dancing the hula with her classmates on the beach in Maui a year or two ago, and I suddenly saw this chain—this genetic link—connecting Serena to her great, great grandmother, my granny Ting. Five generations stretching from that Hawaiian beach all the way back to the wilds of Yorkshire. I thought it was interesting. I thought I'd write some of it down."

"A memoir?" asks Paula. Knowing each other's life stories as we do, she adds, "So are you writing about taking off round the world with a backpack when you were a forty-year-old divorcee? Those drug-crazed horses in Greece? The lover twenty years younger than you? Going to Hawaii for ten days and staying for three years?"

I laugh. "That'll have to be another book."

Just then the dogs jump up and tear off barking madly to greet my English friend Prue's dusty SUV as it comes up the drive. She and Janet, (a.k.a. Miss Canada), get out in a welter of dogs, theirs' and mine. They stroll across the lawn and fling themselves down in the shade.

"This heat!" says Prue. She snatches off her wig and fans herself with it and tosses it over her shoulder. She's half-way through chemotherapy. Her bald head and slender neck make her seem as vulnerable as a child.

I look round at the eager, animated faces of my three dear friends, chattering, laughing, interrupting each other, stroking the dogs.

Between us, I reflect, we've made some disastrous choices and bad marriages, we've had our fair share of adventures, fallen down and picked ourselves up, loved and lost and laughed a lot, and been divorced too many times.

Three of us are currently single.

Two of us have had cancer.

All of us have traveled the world.

Two of us refuse to dye our grey hair.

Three of us have grown-up children we worry about although we know we're not supposed to.

We've all lost people we love.

. . . with one accord we put down our glassess and get up
and embrace Prue, who isn't going to die

I imagine we're pretty representative of our generation.

The wonderful thing is that here we are today, living in what must surely be one of the most beautiful places on earth. And along the way we've grown wise enough to put a high value on friendship, to know we can't fix the world, and to use every day like the precious gift it is.

My husband Dick comes out onto the terrace carrying a tray.

"Bellinis," he announces, putting the tray down on the table and pouring peach juice into five glasses.

Dick and I have just come back from Provence, and Bellinis are our new vice. The champagne cork pops. He hands round the tall bubbly glasses.

Dick

"Don't go!" the women cry but, ever tactful, my lovely husband smiles his gentle smile and takes his glass and goes back through the French doors into the house. He says a male presence changes the dynamics among a group of women, and he's right. He's eight years younger than me, but he's often right.

"I wish we could clone Dick," says Janet, and the others wave their glasses in agreement.

"What shall we drink to?" asks Paula.

"The future?" says Prue. Thanks to the marvels of modern medicine, she has a future.

"Dogs," says Janet. She's so fed up with the men who pursue her that she recently announced she's going to stick to Border Collies.

"Let's drink to this moment," I suggest.

Everyone agrees.

We raise our glasses. "To this moment!"

Then with one accord we put down our glasses and get up and embrace Prue, who isn't going to die.

Four women standing with their arms round each other in a sunny garden. We are surrounded by dogs and humming birds and flowers and bumble-bees and encircled by mountains. Love is in the air.

This woman is aware that she is home at last. And that she is—blessed.

A Recent Gathering of the Beloveds

Dick, grandson Oliver, daughter Jane, me,
granddaughter Serena, daughter Ming, grandson Chimo,
granddaughter Tania, son Steve
Maui 2005

About the Author

Diana Fassino, artist, accidental world traveler, and author of over two hundred published short stories and one novel, lives today in Sun Valley, Idaho.

Her email address is dianafas@cox.net.

978-0-595-39615-3
0-595-39615-1

Printed in the United States
64057LVS00003B/495

9 780595 396153